The Wisdom of
SHAKESPEARE

The Wisdom of
SHAKESPEARE

EDITED BY JOYCE E. HENRY, PH.D.

PHILOSOPHICAL
LIBRARY

CITADEL PRESS
Kensington Publishing Corp.
www.kensingtonbooks.com

CITADEL PRESS BOOKS are published by

Kensington Publishing Corp.
850 Third Avenue
New York, NY 10022

Titles included in the Wisdom Library are published by arrangement with Philosophical Library.

CITADEL PRESS is Reg. U.S. Pat. & TM Off.
The Citadel Logo is a trademark of Kensington Publishing Corp.

First Wisdom Library printing: December 2002

10 9 8 7 6 5 4 3 2 1

Printed in the United States of America

Library of Congress Control Number: 2002110877

ISBN 0-8065-2384-0

CONTENTS

FOREWORD

A man of Renaissance England, William Shakespeare encircles us in the twenty-first century. His plays are constantly in production throughout the world, and his words appear in headlines, editorials, advertisements, book titles, and comic strips. Shakespeare links cultures, centuries, generations, and genders.

Born in Elizabeth I's reign in 1564, William Shakespeare grew up in Stratford-on-Avon, marrying Anne Hathaway from nearby Shottery when he was eighteen and she twenty-six. Few records remain of their first decade together, except for the births of their three children, Susanna, Judith, and Hamnet; but by 1592 Shakespeare was recognized in London as a poet, playwright, and actor. During the next twenty-five years, until his death in 1616, he wrote thirty-seven plays, a canon which includes indisputably the greatest plays in the English language.

The wisdom of Shakespeare shines in the speeches of his characters. Arranged here in rough chronological order by categories, some passages are familiar; some are not. Whether these are truly Shakespeare's thoughts and attitudes, we do not know. Uttered by major and minor characters, and sometimes by those most unsympathetic, these lines reveal Shakespeare's breadth of understanding of the diversity of humankind and his fascination with the motivations that drive behavior. The enormous variety of his expressions is astonishing, and, despite the thousands and thousands of words in his works, he never repeats himself.

The editions used were *The Complete Works of Shakespeare* edited by Hardin Craig and David Bevington (Scott, Foresman, & Co., 1973), and *The Two Noble Kinsmen,* edited by Lois Potter (The Arden Shakespeare, 1997). My appreciation goes to professors Louis A. DeCatur and Rebecca Jaroff for their helpful suggestions.

Use this book to find a message for a friend or loved one, a passage for a special occasion, or simply to read and admire.

ABOUT THE EDITOR

Joyce E. Henry earned her bachelor's degree at the University of Michigan and her master's and doctoral degrees from the University of Wisconsin–Milwaukee. Also a graduate of the Neighborhood Playhouse School of the Theatre in New York City, she worked as an actor, theater manager, and television moderator for a number of years, before joining the English department faculty of Ursinus College in Collegeville, Pennsylvania. As director of the theater program, she mounted more than a dozen Shakespeare productions, as well as *A Matter of Conscience*, her own play based on the life of Fanny Kemble. Currently she performs "Shakespeare's Women" for the Pennsylvania Humanities Council and teaches Shakespeare at the Creutzburg Center in Radnor, Pennsylvania.

KEY TO ABBREVIATIONS
(in chronological order)

The Comedy of Errors	*CE*
Love's Labour's Lost	*LLL*
The Two Gentlemen of Verona	*TGV*
The Taming of the Shrew	*TS*
A Midsummer Night's Dream	*MND*
The First Part of King Henry VI	*1 Henry VI*
The Second Part of King Henry VI	*2 Henry VI*
The Third Part of King Henry VI	*3 Henry VI*
The Tragedy of King Richard III	*Richard III*
The Life and Death of King John	*King John*
Titus Andronicus	*Titus*
Romeo and Juliet	*RJ*
Venus and Adonis	*V&A*
The Merchant of Venice	*MV*
Much Ado About Nothing	*Much Ado*
The Merry Wives of Windsor	*Merry Wives*
As You Like It	*AYLI*
Twelfth Night	*TN*
The Tragedy of King Richard II	*Richard II*
The First Part of King Henry IV	*1 Henry IV*
The Second Part of King Henry IV	*2 Henry IV*
The Life of King Henry V	*Henry V*
Julius Caesar	*JC*
All's Well That Ends Well	*All's Well*
Measure for Measure	*MforM*
Troilus and Cressida	*TC*

Hamlet, Prince of Denmark	*Hamlet*
Othello, the Moor of Venice	*Othello*
King Lear	*Lear*
Timon of Athens	*Timon*
Macbeth	*Macbeth*
Antony and Cleopatra	*A&C*
Coriolanus	*Coriolanus*
Pericles	*Pericles*
Cymbeline	*Cymbeline*
A Winter's Tale	*WT*
The Tempest	*Tempest*
The Famous History of the Life of King Henry VIII	*Henry VIII*
The Two Noble Kinsmen	*TNK*

The Wisdom of
SHAKESPEARE

A

ADVICE: "To thine own self be true"

> Be that thou hop'st to be, or what thou art
> Resign to death; it is not worth th' enjoying.
> > *York—2 Henry VI III.i.*

> First thrash the corn, then after burn the straw.
> > *Demetrius—Titus II.iii*

> Two may keep counsel when the third's away.
> > *Aaron—Titus IV.ii*

> Wisely and slow; they stumble that run fast.
> > *Friar Laurence—RJ II.iii*

Look what thy soul holds dear, imagine it
To lie that way thou goest, not whence thou com'st:
Suppose the singing birds musicians,
The grass whereon thou tread'st the presence strew'd,
The flowers fair ladies, and thy steps no more
Than a delightful measure or a dance;

For gnarling sorrow hath less power to bite
The man that mocks at it and sets it light.
John of Gaunt—Richard II I.iii

When we mean to build,
We first survey the plot, then draw the model;
And when we see the figure of the house,
Then must we rate the cost of the erection;
Which if we find outweighs ability,
What do we then but draw anew the model
In fewer offices, or at last desist
To build at all? *Lord Bardolph—2 Henry IV I.iii*

Be it thy course to busy giddy minds
With foreign quarrels. *King Henry IV—2 Henry IV IV.v*

Love no man in good earnest; nor no further in sport neither than with safety of a pure blush thou mayst in honour come off again. *Celia—AYLI I.ii*

Beware the ides of March.
Soothsayer—JC I.ii

Be absolute for death; either death or life
Shall thereby be the sweeter. Reason thus with life:
If I do lose thee, I do lose a thing
That none but fools would keep: a breath thou art,
Servile to all the skyey influences,
That does this habitation, where thou keep'st,
Hourly afflict: merely, thou art death's fool;
For him thou labour'st by thy flight to shun
And yet runn'st toward him still. *Duke—MforM III.i*

The trifling of his favour,
Hold it a fashion and a toy in blood,
A violet in the youth of primy nature,
Forward, not permanent, sweet, not lasting,
The perfume and suppliance of a minute;
No more.   *Laertes—Hamlet I.iii*

Then weigh what loss your honour may sustain,
If with too credent ear you list his songs,
Or lose your heart, or your chaste treasure open
To his unmast'red importunity.   *Laertes—Hamlet I.iii*

Be wary then: best safety lies in fear:
Youth to itself rebels, though none else near.
                                        Laertes—Hamlet I.iii

These few precepts in thy memory
Look thou character. Give thy thoughts no tongue,
Nor any unproportion'd thought his act.
Be thou familiar, but by no means vulgar.
Those friends thou hast, and their adoption tried,
Grapple them to thy soul with hoops of steel;
But do not dull thy palm with entertainment
Of each new-hatch'd, unfledg'd comrade. Beware
Of entrance to a quarrel, but being in,
Bear't that th' opposed may beware of thee.
Give every man thy ear, but few thy voice;
Take each man's censure, but reserve thy judgment.
Costly thy habit as thy purse can buy,
But not express'd in fancy; rich, not gaudy;
For the apparel oft proclaims the man,
And they in France of the best rank and station
Are of a most select and generous chief in that.

Neither a borrower nor a lender be,
For loan oft loses both itself and friend,
And borrowing dulleth edge of husbandry.
This above all, to thine own self be true,
And it must follow, as the night the day,
Thou canst not then be false to any man.

Polonius—Hamlet I.iii

Assume a virtue, if you have it not.
That monster, custom, who all sense doth eat,
Of habits devil, is angel yet in this,
That to the use of actions fair and good
He likewise gives a frock or livery,
That aptly is put on.   *Hamlet—Hamlet III.iv*

Put money in thy purse; follow thou the wars; defeat thy
favour with an unsurped beard; I say, put money in thy
purse.   *Iago—Othello I.iii*

Know thou this, that men
Are as the time is: to be tender-minded
Does not become a sword.   *Edmund—Lear V.iii*

O, that men's ears should be
To counsel deaf, but not to flattery!   *Apemantus—Timon I.ii*

Things without all remedy
Should be without regard; what's done is done.

Lady Macbeth—Macbeth III.ii

Do not cry havoc, where you should but hunt
With modest warrant.   *Menenius—Coriolanus III.i*

Be advis'd:
Heat not a furnace for your foe so hot
That it do singe yourself: we may outrun,
By violent swiftness, that which we run at,
And lose by over-running.   *Norfolk—Henry VIII I.i*

Where you are liberal of your loves and counsels
Be sure you be not loose; for those you make friends
And give your hearts to, when they once perceive
The least rub in your fortunes, fall away
Like water from ye, never found again
But where they mean to sink ye.
                              Buckingham—Henry VIII II.i

                    I charge thee, fling away ambition:
By that sin fell the angels; how can man, then,
The image of his Maker, hope to win by it?
Love thyself last: cherish those hearts that hate thee;
Corruption wins not more than honesty.
                              Wolsey—Henry VIII III.ii

                    Love and meekness, lord,
Become a churchman better than ambition.
                              Cranmer—Henry VIII V.iii

AGE: "Frosty, but kindly"

Though now this grained face of mine be hid
In sap-consuming winter's drizzled snow
And all the conduits of my blood froze up,
Yet hath my night of life some memory,
My wasting lamps some fading glimmer left,
My dull ears a little use to hear.   *Aegeon—CE V.i*

Why art thou old and want'st experience?
King—2 Henry VI V.i

That time of year thou mayst in me behold,
When yellow leaves, or none, or few do hang
Upon those boughs which shake against the cold,
Bare ruined choirs, where late the sweet birds sang.
In me thou see'st the twilight of such day,
As after sunset fadeth in the west,
Which by and by black night doth take away,
Death's second self that seals up all in rest.
In me thou see'st the glowing of such fire,
That on the ashes of his youth doth lie,
As the death-bed, whereon it must expire,
Consumed with that which it was nourished by.
      This thou perceiv'st, which makes thy love more strong,
      To love that well, which thou must leave ere long.
Sonnet 73

As they say, when the age is in, the wit is out.
Dogberry—Much Ado III.v

For 'tis not good that children should know any wicked-
ness: old folks, you know, have discretion, as they say, and
know the world.   *Quickly—Merry Wives II.i.*

He that doth the ravens feed,
Yea, providently caters for the sparrow,
Be comfort to my age!   *Adam—AYLI II.ii*

      My age is as a lusty winter,
Frosty, but kindly.   *Adam—AYLI II.iii*

At seventeen years many their fortunes seek;
But at fourscore it is too late a week.   *Adam—AYLI II.iii*

You that are old consider not the capacities of us that are
young; you do measure the heat of our livers with the bit-
terness of your galls: and we that are in the vaward of our
youth, I must confess, are wags too.
                                          Falstaff—2 Henry IV I.ii

A man can no more separate age and covetousness than 'a
can part young limbs and lechery: but the gout galls the
one, and the pox pinches the other.
                                          Falstaff—2 Henry IV I.ii

Is it not strange that desire should so many years outlive
performance?   *Poins—2 Henry IV II.iv*

Lord, Lord, how subject we old men are to this vice of lying!
                                          Falstaff—2 Henry IV III.iii

By heaven, it is as proper to our age
To cast beyond ourselves in our opinions
As it is common for the younger sort
To lack discretion.   *Polonius—Hamlet II.i*

The best and soundest of his time hath been but rash; then
must we look from his age to receive not alone the imper-
fections of long-engraffed condition, but therewithal the
unruly waywardness that infirm and choleric years bring
with them.   *Goneril—Lear I .i*

Thou shouldst not have been old till thou hadst been wise.
                                          Fool—Lear I.v

These old fellows
Have their ingratitude in them hereditary:
Their blood is cak'd, 'tis cold, it seldom flows;
'Tis lack of kindly warmth they are not kind;
And nature, as it grows again toward earth,
Is fashion'd for the journey, dull and heavy.

Timon—Timon II.ii

Though age from folly could not give me freedom,
It does from childishness.   *Cleopatra—A&C I.iii*

B

BEASTS AND BIRDS: "No beast so fierce but knows some touch of pity"

O, 'tis a foul thing when a cur cannot keep himself in all companies. *Launce—TGV IV.iv*

The ousel cock so black of hue,
With orange-tawny bill,
The throstle with his note so true,
The wren with little quill—

The finch, the sparrow and the lark,
The plain-song cuckoo gray,
Whose note full many a man doth mark,
And dares not answer nay,—
For, indeed, who would set his will to so foolish a bird?
Bottom—MND III.i

To see how God in all his creatures works!
Yea, man and birds are fain of climbing high.
King—2 Henry VI II.i

Small curs are not regarded when they grin;
But great men tremble when the lion roars.
Queen—2 Henry VI III.i

The fox barks not when he would steal the lamb.

Suffolk—2 Henry VI III.i

The gaudy, blabbing and remorseful day
Is crept into the bosom of the sea;
And now loud-howling wolves arouse the jades
That drag the tragic melancholy night;
Who, with their drowsy, slow and flagging wings,
Clip dead men's graves and from their misty jaws
Breathe foul contagious darkness in the air.

Lieutenant—2 Henry VI IV.i

A staff is quickly found to beat a dog.

Gloucester—2 Henry VI III.i

Drones suck not eagles' blood but rob beehives.

Suffolk—2 Henry VI IV. i

Oft have I seen a hot o'erweening cur
Run back and bite, because he was withheld;
Who, being suffer'd with the bear's fell paw,
Hath clapp'd his tail between his legs and cried.

Richard—2 Henry VI V.i

So looks the pent-up lion o'er the wretch
That trembles under his devouring paws;
And so he walks, insulting o'er his prey,
And so he comes, to rend his limbs asunder.

Rutland—3 Henry VI I.iii

I have seen a swan
With bootless labour swim against the tide
And spend her strength with over-matching waves.

York—3 Henry VI I.iv

To whom do lions cast their gentle looks?
Not to the beast that would usurp their den.
Whose hand is that the forest bear doth lick?
Not his that spoils her young before her face.
Who 'scapes the lurking serpent's mortal sting?
Not he that sets his foot upon her back.
The smallest worm will turn being trodden on,
And doves will peck in safeguard of their brood.

Clifford—3 Henry VI II.ii

Unreasonable creatures feed their young;
And though man's face be fearful to their eyes,
Yet, in protection of their tender ones,
Who hath not seen them, even with those wings
Which sometime they have us'd with fearful flight,
Offering their own lives in their young's defence?

Clifford—3 Henry VI II.ii

But when the fox hath once got in his nose,
He'll soon find means to make the body follow.

Gloucester—3 Henry VI IV.vii

No beast so fierce but knows some touch of pity.

Anne—Richard III I.ii

The world is grown so bad,
That wrens make prey where eagles dare not perch.

Gloucester—Richard III I.iii

The lion mov'd with pity did endure
To have his princely paws par'd away.   *Lavinia—Titus II.iii*

Weke, weke! so cries a pig prepared to the spit.

Aaron—Titus IV.ii

The eagle suffers little birds to sing,
And is not careful what they mean thereby,
Knowing that with the shadow of his wings
He can at pleasure stint their melody.   *Tamora—Titus IV.iv*

But where the bull and cow are both milk-white,
They never do beget a coal-black calf.

Second Goth—Titus V.i

For the ewe that will not hear her lamb when it baes will
never answer a calf when he bleats.

Dogberry—Much Ado III.iii

When night-dogs run, all sorts of deer are chas'd.

Falstaff—Merry Wives V.v

Hope is a curtal dog in some affairs

Pistol—Merry Wives II.i

O world, how apt the poor are to be proud!
If one should be a prey, how much the better
To fall before the lion than the wolf!   *Olivia—TN III.i*

Lions make leopards tame.

King Richard—Richard II I.i

The lion dying thrusteth forth his paw,
And wounds the earth, if nothing else, with rage
To be o'erpow'r'd.   *Queen—Richard II V.i*

O, the blood more stirs
To rouse a lion than to start a hare!

Hotspur—1 Henry IV I.iii

For treason is but trusted like the fox,
Who, ne'er so tame, so cherish'd and lock'd up,
Will have a wild trick of his ancestors.

Worcester—1 Henry IV V.ii

The times are wild; contention, like a horse
Full of high feeding, madly hath broke loose
And bears down all before him.

Northumberland—2 Henry IV I.i

To wake a wolf is as bad as smell a fox.

Falstaff—2 Henry IV I.ii

You may stroke him as gently as a puppy greyhound: he'll
not swagger with a Barbary hen, if her feathers turn back in
any show of resistance.   *Falstaff—2 Henry IV II.iv*

Let gallows gape for dog; let man go free
And let not hemp his wind-pipe suffocate.

Pistol—Henry V III.vi

Foolish curs, that run winking into the mouth of a Russian
bear and have their heads crushed like rotten apples! You
may as well say, that's a valiant flea that dare eat his breakfast on the lip of a lion.   *Orleans—Henry V III.vii*

The man that once did sell the lion's skin
While the beast liv'd, was kill'd with hunting him.

King Henry—Henry V IV.iii

It is the bright day that brings forth the adder;
And that craves wary walking.   *Brutus—JC II.i*

Two curs shall tame each other: pride alone
Must tarre the mastiffs on, as 'twere a bone. *Nestor—TC I.iii*

The elephant hath joints, but none for courtesy; his legs are
legs for necessity, not for flexure.   *Ulysses—TC II.iii*

Truth's a dog must to kennel; he must be whipped out,
when Lady the brach may stand by the fire and stink
Fool—Lear I.iv

Avaunt, you curs!
Be thy mouth or black or white,
Tooth that poisons if it bite;
Mastiff, greyhound, mongrel grim,
Hound or spaniel, brach or lym,
Or bobtail tike or trundle-tail,
Tom will make him weep and wail:
For, with throwing thus my head,
Dogs leap'd the hatch, and all are fled.   *Edgar—Lear III.vi*

He's mad that trusts in the tameness of a wolf, a horse's
health, a boy's love, or a whore's oath.   *Fool—Lear III.vi*

If thou wert the lion, the fox would beguile thee; If thou
wert the lamb, the fox would eat thee; if thou wert the fox,
the lion would suspect thee, when peradventure thou wert
accused by the ass: if thou wert the ass, thy dulness would
torment thee, and still thou livest but as a breakfast to the
wolf: if thou wert the wolf, thy greediness would afflict
thee, and oft thou shouldst hazard thy life for thy dinner;
wert thou the unicorn, pride and wrath would confound
thee and make thine own self the conquest of thy fury; wert
thou a bear, thou wouldst be killed by the horse; wert thou
a horse, thou wouldst be seized by the leopard: wert thou a

leopard, thou wert german to the lion and the spots of thy kindred were jurors on thy life: all thy safety were remotion and thy defence absence. What beast couldst thou be, that were not subject to a beast? *Timon—Timon IV.iii*

This guest of summer,
The temple-haunting martlet, does approve,
By his lov'd mansionry, that the heaven's breath
Smells wooingly here; no jutty, frieze,
Buttress, nor coign of vantage, but this bird
Hath made his pendent bed and procreant cradle;
Where they most breed and haunt, I have observ'd,
The air is delicate. *Banquo—Macbeth I.vi*

In the catalogue ye go for men,
As hounds and greyhounds, mongrels, spaniels, curs,
Shoughs, water-rugs and demi-wolves are clept
All be the name of dogs: the valued file
Distinguishes the swift, the slow, the subtle,
The housekeeper, the hunter, every one
According to the gift which bounteous nature
Hath to him clos'd, whereby he does receive
Particular addition from the bill
That writes them all alike: and so of men.
Macbeth—Macbeth III.i

'Tis better playing with a lion's whelp
Than with an old one dying. *Enobarbus—A&C III.xiii*

Nature teaches beasts to know their friends.
Sicinius—Coriolanus II.i

You know, strange fowl light upon neighboring ponds.
Iachimo—Cymbeline I.iv

This butcher's cur is venom-mouth'd, and I
Have not the power to muzzle him.

Buckingham—Henry VIII I.i

   Those that tame wild horses
Pace 'em not in their hands to make 'em gentle,
But stop their mouths with stubborn bits, and spur 'em,
Till they obey the manage.   *Gardiner—Henry VIII V.iii*

   You play the spaniel,
And think with wagging of your tongue to win me.

King—Henry VIII V.iii

BEAUTY: "What doth her beauty serve?"

Beauty is bought by judgement of the eye,
Not utter'd by base sale of chapmen's tongues.

Princess—LLL II.i

   And the old saying is,
Black men are pearls in beauteous ladies' eyes.

Proteus—TGV V.ii

O, she is rich in beauty, only poor,
That when she dies, with beauty dies her store.

Romeo—RJ I.i

For beauty starv'd with her severity
Cuts beauty off from all posterity.   *Romeo—RJ I.i*

Show me a mistress that is passing fair,
What doth her beauty serve, but as a note
Where I may read who pass'd that passing fair?

Romeo—RJ I.i

Her beauty makes
This vault a feasting presence full of light.   *Romeo—RJ V.ii*

Make use of time, let not advantage slip;
Beauty within itself should not be wasted:
Fair flowers that are not gath'red in their prime
Rot and consume themselves in little time.
Venus—V&A 29–32

Beauty provoketh thieves sooner than gold.
Rosalind—AYLI I.iii

Honesty coupled to beauty is to have honey a sauce to sugar.
Touchstone—AYLI III.iii

'Tis beauty truly blent, whose red and white
Nature's own sweet and cunning hand laid on.
Viola—TN I.v

O beauty! where is thy faith?
Troilus—TC V.ii

For the power of beauty will sooner transform honesty from
what it is to a bawd than the force of honesty can translate
beauty into his likeness.   *Hamlet—Hamlet III.i*

The beauty that is borne here in the face
The bearer knows not, but commends itself
To others' eyes; nor doth the eye itself,
That most pure spirit of sense, behold itself,
Not going from itself; but eye to eye oppos'd
Salutes each other with each other's form;
For speculation turns not to itself,
Till it hath travell'd and is mirror'd there
Where it may see itself.   *Achilles—TC III.iii*

BEHAVIOUR: "Action is eloquence"

To move is to stir; and to be valiant is to stand: therefore, if
thou art moved, thou runn'st away.   *Gremio—RJ I.i*

> He jests at scars, that never felt a wound.
>   *Romeo—RJ II.ii*

But fish not with this melancholy bait,
For this fool gudgeon, this opinion.   *Gratiano—MV I.i*

In my school-days, when I had lost one shaft,
I shot his fellow of the self-same flight
The self-same way with more advised watch,
To find the other forth, and by adventuring both
I oft found both.   *Bassanio—MV I.i*

How much better is it to weep at joy than to joy at weeping!
    Leonato—Much Ado I.i

Ho! now you strike like the blind man: 'twas the boy that
stole your meat, and you'll beat the post.
    Benedick—Much Ado II.i

> They that touch pitch will be defiled.
>   *Dogberry—Much Ado III.iii*

God's a good man; an two men ride of a horse, one, must
ride behind.   *Dogberry—Much Ado III.v*

> Fashion wears out more apparel than the man.
>   *Conrad—Much Ado III.iii*

'Tis all men's office to speak patience
To those that wring under the load of sorrow,
But no man's virtue nor sufficiency
To be so moral when he shall endure
The like himself.   *Leonato—Much Ado V.i*

I do despise a liar as I do despise one that is false, or as I despise one that is not true.   *Evans—Merry Wives I.i*

Those that are good manners at the court are as ridiculous in the country as the behaviour of the country is most mockable at the court.   *Corin—AYLI III.ii*

I'm sure care's an enemy to life
                    Sir Toby—TN I.iii

These clothes are good enough to drink in; and so be these boots too: an they be not, let them hang themselves in their own straps.   *Sir Toby—TN I.iii*

Wise men ne'er sit and wail their woes,
But presently prevent the ways to wail.
                    Carlisle—Richard II III.ii

For do we must what force will have us do.
                    King Richard—Richard II III.iii

Falstaff sweats to death,
And lards the lean earth as he walks along.
                    Prince—1 Henry IV II.ii

There is nothing but roguery to be found in villanous man: yet a coward is worse than a cup of sack with lime in it.
                    Falstaff—1 Henry IV II.iv

It is certain that either wise bearing or ignorant carriage is caught, as men take diseases, one of another; therefore let men take heed of their company.   *Falstaff—2 Henry IV V.i*

But 'tis a common proof,
That lowliness is young ambition's ladder,
Whereto the climber-upward turns his face;
But when he once attains the upmost round,
He then unto the ladder turns his back,
Looks in the clouds, scorning the base degrees
By which he did ascend.   *Brutus—JC II.i*

Who cannot be crushed with a plot?
    Parolles—All's Well IV.iii

Our doubts are traitors
And make us lose the good we oft might win
By fearing to attempt.   *Lucio—MforM I.iv*

Those wounds heal ill that men do give themselves:
Omission to do what is necessary
Seals a commission to a blank of danger;
And danger, like an ague, subtly taints
Even then when we sit idly in the sun.
    Patroclus—TC III.iii

O, sir, to such as boasting show their scars
A mock is due.   *Troilus—TC IV.v*

Let the candied tongue lick absurd pomp,
And crook the pregnant hinges of the knee
Where thrift may follow fawning.   *Hamlet—Hamlet III.ii*

> Let it work;
> For 'tis the sport to have the enginer
> Hoist with his own petar.   *Hamlet—Hamlet III.iv*

> Knavery's plain face is never seen till us'd.
> *Iago—Othello II.i*

This is the excellent foppery of the world, that when we are sick in fortune, often the surfeits of our own behavior, we make guilty of our disasters the sun, the moon and stars: as if we were villains on necessity, fools by heavenly compulsion; knaves, thieves and treachers, by spherical predominance; drunkards, liars and adulterers, by an enforced obedience of planetary influence, and all that we are evil in, by a divine thrusting on: an admirable evasion of whoremaster man, to lay his goatish disposition on the charge of a star!   *Edmund—Lear I.ii*

> Come, let's away to prison:
> We two alone will sing like birds i' the cage:
> When thou dost ask me blessing, I'll kneel down,
> And ask of thee forgiveness: so we'll live,
> And pray, and sing, and tell old tales, and laugh
> As gilded butterflies, and hear poor rogues
> Talk of court news; and we'll talk with them too,
> Who loses and who wins; who's in, who's out;
> And take upon's the mystery of things,
> As if we were God's spies: and we'll wear out,
> In a wall'd prison, packs and sects of great ones,
> That ebb and flow by th' moon.   *Lear—Lear V.iii*

> The attempt and not the deed
> Confounds us.   *Lady Macbeth—Macbeth II.ii*

Celerity is never more admir'd
Than by the negligent.   *Cleopatra—A&C III.vii*

Action is eloquence, and the eyes of th' ignorant
More learned than the ears.   *Volumnia—Coriolanus III.ii*

                    One good deed dying tongueless
Slaughters a thousand waiting upon that.
                                        Hermione—WT I.ii

            Misery acquaints a man with strange bedfellows.
                                        Caliban—Tempest II.ii

Tongues spit their duties out, and cold hearts freeze
Allegiance in them; their curses now
Live where their prayers did.   *Katharine—Henry VIII I.ii*

                    'Tis in our power,
Unless we fear that apes can tutor's, to
Be masters of our manners.   *Palamon—TNK I.ii*

C

CONSCIENCE: "It is a dangerous thing"

The worm of conscience still begnaw thy soul!
Queen Margaret—Richard III I.iii

It is a dangerous thing; it makes a man a coward: a man cannot steal, but it accuseth him; a man cannot swear, but it checks him; a man cannot lie with his neighbour's wife, but it detects him: 'tis a blushing shamefac'd spirit that mutinies in a man's bosom; it fills a man full of obstacles: it made me once restore a purse of gold that by chance I found; it beggars any man that keeps it; it is turned out of towns and cities for a dangerous thing; and every man that means to live well endeavours to trust to himself and live without it. *Second Murderer—Richard III I.iv*

Every man's conscience is a thousand men,
To fight against this guilty homicide.
Richmond—Richard III V.ii

My conscience hath a thousand several tongues,
And every tongue brings in a several tale,
And every tale condemns me for a villain.
Richard—Richard III V.iii

Conscience is but a word that cowards use,
Devis'd at first to keep the strong in awe:
Our strong arms be our conscience, swords our law.
King Richard—Richard III V.iv

The guilt of conscience take thou for thy labour,
But neither my good word nor princely favour;
With Cain go wander through shades of night,
And never show thy head by day nor light.
Bolingbroke—Richard II V.vi

How smart a lash that speech doth give my conscience!
The harlot's cheek, beautied with plast'ring art,
Is not more ugly to the thing that helps it
Than is my deed to my most painted word.
Claudius—Hamlet III.i

So full of artless jealousy is guilt,
It spills itself in fearing to be spilt.   *Gertrude—Hamlet IV.v*

Men must learn now with pity to dispense;
For policy sits above conscience.
First Stranger—Timon III.ii

I feel within me
A peace above all earthly dignities,
A still and quiet conscience.   *Wolsey—Henry VIII III.ii*

THE CROWN: "O polished perturbation! golden care!

Do but think
How sweet a thing it is to wear a crown;

Within whose circuit is Elysium
And all that poets feign of bliss and joy.

Richard—3 Henry VI I.ii

My crown is in my heart, not in my head;
Not deck'd with diamonds and Indian stones,
Not to be seen: my crown is called content:
A crown it is that seldom kings enjoy.

King—3 Henry VI III.i

I'll make my heaven to dream upon the crown,
And, whiles I live, t' account this world but hell,
Until my mis-shap'd trunk that bears this head
Be round impaled with a glorious crown

Gloucester—3 Henry VI III.ii

A sceptre snatch'd with an unruly hand
Must be as boisterously maintain'd as gain'd;
And he that stands upon a slipp'ry place
Makes nice of no vile hold to stay him up.

Pandulph—King John III.iv

A thousand flatterers sit within thy crown,
Whose compass is no bigger than thy head;
And yet, incaged in so small a verge
The waste is no whit lesser than thy land.

John of Gaunt—Richard II II.i

Not all the water in the rough rude sea
Can wash the balm off from an anointed king;
The breath of worldly men cannot depose
The deputy elected by the Lord.

King Richard—Richard II III.ii

Why doth the crown lie there upon his pillow,
Being so troublesome a bedfellow?
O polish'd perturbation! golden care!
That keep'st the ports of slumber open wide
To many a watchful night!

Prince—2 Henry IV IV. v

I know
'Tis not the balm, the sceptre and the ball,
The sword, the mace, the crown imperial,
The intertissued robe of gold and pearl,
The farced titled running 'fore the king,
The throne he sits on, nor the tide of pomp
That beats upon the high shore of this world,
No, not all these, thrice-gorgeous ceremony,
Not all these, laid in bed majestical,
Can sleep so soundly as the wretched slave,
Who with a body fill'd and vacant mind
Gets him to rest, cramm'd with distressful bread;
Never sees horrid night, the child of hell,
But, like a lackey, from the rise to set
Sweats in the eye of Phoebus and all night
Sleeps in Elysium; next day after dawn,
Doth rise and help Hyperion to his horse,
And follows so the ever-running year,
With profitable labour, to his grave:
And, but for ceremony, such a wretch,
Winding up days with toil and nights with sleep,
Had the forehand and vantage of a king.

King Henry—Henry V IV.i

There's such divinity doth hedge a king,
That treason can but peep to what it would,
Acts little of his will.
Claudius—Hamlet IV.v

D

DREAMS: "Children of an idle brain"

I have had a most rare vision. I have had a dream, past the wit of man to say what dream it was: man is but an ass, if he go about to expound this dream. Methought I was—there is no man can tell what. Methought I was—and methought I had—but man is a patched fool, if he will offer to say what methought I had. The eye of man hath not heard, the ear of man hath not seen, man's hand is not able to taste, his tongue to conceive, nor his heart to report, what my dream was.   *Bottom—MND IV.i*

                        True, I talk of dreams,
Which are the children of an idle brain,
Begot of nothing but vain fantasy,
Which is as thin of substance as the air
And more inconstant than the wind, who wooes
Even now the frozen bosom of the north,
And, being angered, puffs away from thence,
Turning his side to the dew-dropping south.
                                    Mercutio—RJ I.iv

What relish is in this? how runs the stream?
Or I am mad, or else this is a dream:
Let fancy still my sense in Lethe sleep;
If it be thus to dream, still let me sleep!   *Sebastian—TN IV.i*

I know thee not, old man: fall to thy prayers;
How ill white hairs become a fool and jester!
I have long dream'd of such a kind of man,
So surfeit-swell'd, so old and so profane;
But, being awak'd, I do despise my dream.

King Henry V—2 Henry IV V.v

O God, I could be bounded in a nutshell and count myself a
king of infinite space, were it not that I have bad dreams.

Hamlet—Hamlet II.ii

I dream'd there was an Emperor Antony:
O, such another sleep, that I might see
But such another man!   *Cleopatra—A&C V.ii*

This is the rarest dream that e'er dull sleep
Did mock sad fools withal.   *Pericles—Pericles V.i*

　　　　　Poor wretches that depend
On greatness' favour dream as I have done,
Wake and find nothing. But, alas, I swerve:
Many dream not to find, neither deserve,
And yet are steep'd in favours; so am I,
That have this golden chance and know not why.

Posthumus—Cymbeline V.iv

My life stands in the level of your dreams,
Which I'll lay down.   *Hermione—WT III.i*

　　　　　Dreams are toys;
Yet for this once, yea, superstitiously,
I will be squar'd by this.   *Antigonus—WT III.iii*

E

EDUCATION: "O, what learning is!"

Study is like the heaven's glorious sun
That will not be deep-search'd with saucy looks:
Small have continual plodders ever won
Save base authority from others' books.
These earthly godfathers of heaven's lights
That give a name to every fixed star
Have no more profit of their shining nights
Than those that walk and wot not what they are.
Too much to know is to know nought but fame;
And every godfather can give a name.   *Berowne—LLL I.i*

O thou monster Ignorance, how deformed dost thou look!
                                    Holofernes—LLL IV.ii

Sir, he hath never fed of the dainties that are bred in a book;
he hath not eat paper, as it were; he hath not drunk ink: his
intellect is not replenished; he is only an animal, only sensible in the duller parts.   *Nathaniel—LLL IV.ii*

No profit grows where is no pleasure ta'en;
In brief, sir, study what you most affect.   *Tranio—TS I.i*

O, this learning, what a thing it is!
                                    Gremio—TS I.ii

Thou hast most traitorously corrupted the youth of the realm in erecting a grammar school: and whereas, before, our forefathers had no other books but the score and the tally, thou hast caused printing to be used, and, contrary to the king, his crown and dignity, thou hast built a paper-mill. It will be proved that thou hast men about thee that usually talk of a noun and a verb, and such abominable words as no Christian ear can endure.

Cade—2 Henry VI IV.vii

O Lord, I could have stay'd here all the night
To hear good counsel. O, what learning is!   *Nurse—RJ III.iii*

To be a well-favoured man is the gift of fortune; but to write and read comes by nature.   *Dogberry—Much Ado III.iii*

You do ill to teach the child such words: he teaches him to hick and to hack, which they'll do fast enough of themselves, and to call 'horum:' fie upon you!

Quickly—Merry Wives IV.i

I say, there is no darkness but ignorance, in which thou art more puzzled than the Egyptians in their fog.

Feste—TN IV.ii

The prince but studies his companions
Like a strange tongue, wherein, to gain the language,
'Tis needful that the most immodest word
Be look'd upon and learn'd; which once attain'd,
Your highness knows, comes to no further use
But to be known and hated.   *Warwick—2 Henry IV IV.iv*

I had rather be a tick in a sheep than such a valiant ignorance.

Thersites—TC III.iii

Those that do teach young babes
Do it with gentle means and easy tasks.
Desdemona—Othello IV.ii

O, sir, to willful men,
The injuries that they themselves procure
Must be their schoolmasters.   Regan—Lear II.iv

When thou cam'st first,
Thou strok'st me and made much of me, wouldst give me
Water with berries in 't, and teach me how
To name the bigger light, and how the less,
That burn by day and night: and then I lov'd thee
And show'd thee all the qualities o' th' isle,
The fresh springs, brine-pits, barren place and fertile:
Curs'd be I that did so!   Caliban—Tempest I.ii

You taught me language; and my profit on 't
Is, I know how to curse. The red plague rid you
For learning me your language!   Caliban—Tempest I.ii

EVIL: "Can the devil speak true?"

Marry, he must have a long spoon that must eat with the
devil.   Dromio of Syracuse—CE IV.iii

I always thought
It was both impious and unnatural
That such immanity and bloody strife
Should reign among professors of one faith.
King—1 Henry VI V.i

They say, 'A crafty knave does need no broker.'

Hume—2 Henry VI I.ii

Wizards know their times:
Deep night, dark night, the silent of the night,
The time of night when Troy was set on fire;
The time when screech-owls cry and ban-dogs howl
And spirits walk and ghosts break up their graves,
That time best fits the work we have in hand.

Bolingbroke—2 Henry VI I.iv

O God, what mischiefs work the wicked ones,
Heaping confusion on their own heads thereby!

King—2 Henry VI II.i

How oft the sight of means to do ill deeds
Make deeds ill done!   *King John—King John IV.ii*

O nature, what hadst thou to do in hell,
When thou didst bower the spirit of a fiend
In mortal paradise of such sweet flesh?   *Juliet—RJ III.ii*

The devil can cite Scripture for his purpose;
An evil soul producing holy witness
Is like a villain with a smiling cheek,
A goodly apple rotten at the heart:
O, what a goodly outside falsehood hath!

Antonio—MV I.iii

I like not fair terms and a villain's mind.

Bassanio—MV I.iii

I never did repent for doing good.

Portia—MV III.iv

O, what authority and show of truth
Can cunning sin cover itself withal!
Claudio—Much Ado IV.i

    Fie on sinful fantasy!
    Fie on lust and luxury!
Lust is but a bloody fire,
Kindled with unchaste desire,
Fed in heart, whose flames aspire
As thought do blow them, higher and higher.
Quickly—Merry Wives V.v

What, man? defy the devil: consider, he's an enemy to mankind.
Sir Toby—TN III.iv

What, man! 'tis not for gravity to play at cherry-pit with Satan: hang him, foul collier!
Sir Toby—TN III.iv

In nature there's no blemish but the mind;
None can be call'd deform'd but the unkind;
Virtue is beauty, but the beauteous evil
Are empty trunks o'erflourished by the devil.
Antonio—TN III.iv

    He will give the devil his due.
Prince—1 Henry IV I.ii

O, while you live, tell truth and shame the devil.
Hotspur—1 Henry IV III.i

There is some soul of goodness in things evil,
Would men observingly distil it out.
For our bad neighbour makes us early stirrers,
Which is both healthful and good husbandry:

Besides, they are our outward consciences,
And preachers to us all, admonishing
That we should dress us fairly for our end.
Thus may we gather honey from the weed,
And make a moral of the devil himself.

King Henry—Henry V IV.i

I am a woodland fellow, sir, that always loved a great fire;
and the master I speak of ever keeps a good fire. But, sure,
he is the prince of the world; let his nobility remain in 's
court. I am for the house with the narrow gate, which I take
to be too little for pomp to enter: some that humble themselves may; but the many will be too chill and tender, and
they'll be for the flowery way that leads to the broad gate
and the great fire.   Clown—All's Well IV.v

Foul deeds will rise,
Though all the earth o'erwhelm them, to men's eyes.

Hamlet—Hamlet I.ii

For murder, though it have no tongue, will speak
With most miraculous organ.   Hamlet—Hamlet II.ii

We are oft to blame in this—
'Tis too much prov'd—that with devotion's visage
And pious action we do sugar o'er
The devil himself.   Polonius—Hamlet III.i

It is engend'red. Hell and night
Must bring this monstrous birth to the world's light.

Iago—Othello I.iii

O thou invisible spirit of wine, if thou hast no name
to be known by, let us call thee devil!   Cassio—Othello II.iii

To be now a sensible man, by and by a fool, and presently a beast! O strange! Every inordinate cup is unblessed and the ingredient is a devil.

Cassio—Othello II.iii

Divinity of hell!
When devils will the blackest sins put on,
They do suggest at first with heavenly shows,
As I do now.

Iago—Othello II.iii

A horned man's a monster and a beast.

Othello—Othello IV.i

Villany hath made mocks with love.

Emilia—Othello V.ii

The devil knew not what he did when he made man politic; he crossed himself by 't: and I cannot think but, in the end, the villanies of man will set him clear.

Servant—Timon III.iii

Fillet of a fenny snake,
In the cauldron boil and bake;
Eye of newt and toe of frog,
Wool of bat and tongue of dog,
Adder's fork and blind-worm's sting,
Lizard's leg and howlet's wing,
For a charm of pow'rful trouble,
Like a hell broth boil and bubble.

Second Witch—Macbeth IV.i

By the pricking of my thumbs,
Something wicked this way comes.

Second Witch—Macbeth IV.i

What, can the devil speak true?

Banquo—Macbeth I.iii

'Tis strange,
And oftentimes, to win us to our harm,
The instruments of darkness tell us truths,
Win us with honest trifles, to betray's
In deepest consequence.   *Banquo—Macbeth I.iii*

Better be with the dead,
Whom we, to gain our peace, have sent to peace,
Than on the torture of the mind to lie
In restless ecstasy.   *Macbeth—Macbeth III.ii*

The time has been,
That, when the brains were out, the man would die,
And there an end; but now they rise again,
With twenty mortal murders on their crowns,
And push us from our stools: this is more strange
Than such a murder is.   *Macbeth—Macbeth III.iv*

It will have blood; they say, blood will have blood:
Stones have been known to move and trees to speak;
Augurs and understood relations have
By magot-pies and choughs and rooks brought forth
The secret'st man of blood.   *Macbeth—Macbeth III.iv*

You must not think I am so simple but I know the devil himself will not eat a woman: I know that a woman is a dish for the gods, if the devil dress her not. But, truly, these same whoreson devils do the gods great harm in their women; for in every ten that they make, the devils mar five.

Clown—A&C V.ii

Few love to hear the sins they love to act.

Pericles—Pericles I.i

One sin, I know, another doth provoke,
Murder's as near to lust as flame to smoke.
Poison and treason are the hands of sin,
Ay, and the targets, to put off the shame.

Pericles—Pericles I.i

    Ye're like one that superstitiously
Do swear to th' gods that winter kills the flies.

Dionyza—Pericles IV.iii

This is a devil and no monster: I will leave him; I
have no long spoon.   *Stephano—Tempest II.ii*

The devil speed him! no man's pie is freed
From his ambitious finger.   *Buckingham—Henry VIII I.i*

  Affairs, that walk,
As they say spirits do, at midnight, have
In them a wilder nature than the business
That seeks dispatch by day.   *Gardiner—Henry VIII V.i*

F

FATHERS, MOTHERS, AND SIBLINGS:
"Our house is hell"

To you your father should be as a god.
Theseus—MND I.i

Didst thou never hear
That things ill-got had ever bad success?
And happy always was it for that son
Whose father for his hoarding went to hell?
King—3 Henry VI II.ii

It is a wise father that knows his own child.
Launcelot—MV II.ii

Our house is hell, and thou, a merry devil,
Didst rob it of some taste of tediousness.   *Jessica—MV II.iii*

I know you are my eldest brother, and, in the gentle condition of blood, you should so know me. The courtesy of nations allows you my better, in that you are the first-born; but the same tradition takes not away my blood, were there twenty brothers betwixt us; I have as much of my father in me as you; albeit, I confess, your coming before me is nearer to his reverence.
Orlando—AYLI I.i

Finds brotherhood in thee no sharper spur?
Hath love in thy old blood no living fire?

Duchess—Richard II I.ii

Can no man tell me of my unthrifty son?
'Tis full three months since I did see him last:
If any plague hang over us, 'tis he.

Bolingbroke—Richard II V.iii

That thou art my son, I have partly thy mother's word,
partly my own opinion, but chiefly a villanous trick of thine
eye and a foolish-hanging of thy nether lip, that doth warrant me.   *Falstaff—1 Henry IV II.iv*

Most subject is the fattest soil to weeds;
And he, the noble image of my youth,
Is overspread with them.   *King—2 Henry IV IV.iv*

See, sons, what things you are!
How quickly nature falls into revolt
When gold becomes her object!
For this the foolish over-careful fathers
Have broke their sleep with thoughts, their brains with
    care,
Their bones with industry;
For this they have engrossed and pil'd up
The cank'red heaps of strange-achieved gold;
For this they have been thoughtful to invest
Their sons with arts and martial exercises:
When, like the bee, tolling from every flower
The virtuous sweets,
Our thighs pack'd with wax, our mouths with honey,
We bring it to the hive, and, like the bees,

Are murd'red for our pains. This bitter taste
Yield his engrossments to the ending father.

King—2 Henry IV IV.v

A little more than kin, and less than kind.

Hamlet—Hamlet I.ii

Do not for ever with thy vailed lids
Seek for thy noble father in the dust:
Thou know'st 'tis common; all that lives must die,
Passing through nature to eternity.   *Gertrude—Hamlet I.ii*

But, you must know, your father lost a father;
That father lost, lost his, and the survivor bound
In filial obligation for some term
To do obsequious sorrow.   *Claudius—Hamlet I.ii*

My noble father,
To you I am bound for life and education;
My life and education both do learn me
How to respect you: you are the lord of duty;
I am hitherto your daughter: but here's my husband,
And so much duty as my mother show'd
To you, preferring you before her father,
So much I challenge that I may profess
Due to the Moor my lord.   *Desdemona—Othello I.iii*

O treason of the blood!
Fathers, from hence trust not your daughters' minds
By what you see them act.   *Brabantio—Othello I.i*

I know you what you are;
And like a sister am most loath to call
Your faults as they are nam'd.   *Cordelia—Lear I.i*

Ingratitude, thou marble-hearted fiend,
More hideous when thou show'st thee in a child
Than the sea-monster!   *Lear—Lear I.iv*

                    If she must teem,
Create her child of spleen; that it may live,
And be a thwart disnatur'd torment to her!
Let it stamp wrinkles in her brow of youth;
With cadent tears fret channels in her cheeks;
Turn all her mother's pains and benefits
To laughter and contempt; that she may feel
How sharper than a serpent's tooth it is
To have a thankless child!   *Lear—Lear I.iv*

        Fathers that wear rags
        Do make their children blind;
        But fathers that bear bags
        Shall see their children kind.
        Fortune, that arrant whore,
        Ne'er turns the key to th' poor.   *Fool—Lear II.iv*

            Come all to ruin; let
Thy mother rather feel thy pride than fear
Thy dangerous stoutness, for I mock at death
With as big heart as thou. Do as thou list,
Thy valiantness was mine, thou suck'dst it from me,
But owe thy pride thyself.   *Volumnia—Coriolanus III.ii*

Come, leave your tears: a brief farewell: the beast
With many heads butts me away. Nay, mother,
Where is your ancient courage? You were us'd
To say extremities was the trier of spirits;
That common chances common men could bear;
That when the sea was calm all boats alike

Show'd mastership in floating; fortune's blows,
When, most struck home, being gentle wounded, craves
A noble cunning: you were us'd to load me
With precepts that would make invincible
The heart that conn'd them.   *Coriolanus—Coriolanus IV.i*

O noble strain!
O worthiness of nature! breed of greatness!
Cowards father cowards and base things are base:
Nature hath meal and bran, contempt and grace.
                              Belarius—Cymbeline IV.ii

I would there were no age between sixteen and three-and-
twenty, or that youth would sleep out the rest: for there is
nothing in the between but getting wenches with child,
wronging the ancientry, stealing, fighting.
                              Shepherd—WT III.iii

Kings are no less unhappy, their issue not being gracious,
than they are in losing them when they have approved their
virtues.   *Polixenes—WT IV.ii*

Reason my son
Should choose himself a wife, but as good reason
The father, all whose joy is nothing else
But fair posterity, should hold some counsel
In such a business.   *Polixenes— WT IV.iv*

Good wombs have borne bad sons.
                              Miranda—Tempest I.ii

But, O, how oddly will it sound that I
Must ask my child forgiveness!   *Alonso—Tempest V.i*

FORTUNE AND FATE: "Out, out, thou strumpet, Fortune!"

>   Yield not thy neck
> To fortune's yoke, but let thy dauntless mind
> Still ride in triumph over all mischance.
> > *Lewis—3 Henry VI III.iii*

> Though fortune's malice overthrow my state,
> My mind exceeds the compass of her wheel.
> > *King Edward—3 Henry VI IV.iii*

> What fates impose, that men must needs abide;
> It boots not to resist both wind and tide.
> > *King Edward—3 Henry VI IV.iii*

>   All unavoided is the doom of destiny.
> > *Richard—Richard III IV.iv*

> No, no, when Fortune means to men most good,
> She looks upon them with a threat'ning eye.
> > *Pandulph—King John III.iv*

>   O, I am fortune's fool!
> > *Romeo—RJ III.i*

> O Fortune, Fortune! All men call thee fickle:
> If thou art fickle, what does thou with him
> That is renown'd for faith?   *Juliet—RJ III.v*

> If Fortune be a woman, she's a good wench for this gear.
> > *Launcelot—MV II.ii*

Grieve not that I am fall'n to this for you;
For herein Fortune shows herself more kind
Than is her custom; it is still her use
To let the wretched man outlive his wealth,
To view with hollow eye and wrinkled brow
An age of poverty; from which ling'ring penance
Of such misery doth she cut me off.   *Antonio—MV IV.i*

Let us sit and mock the good housewife Fortune from her
wheel, that her gifts may henceforth be bestowed equally.
Celia—AYLI I.ii

Fortune reigns in gifts of the world, not in the lineaments of
Nature.   *Rosalind—AYLI I.ii*

O God! that one might read the book of fate,
And see the revolution of the times
Make mountains level, and the continent,
Weary of solid firmness, melt itself
Into the sea!   *King—2 Henry IV III.i*

Will Fortune never come with both hands full,
But write her fair words still in foulest letters?
She either gives a stomach and no food;
Such are the poor, in health; or else a feast
And takes away the stomach; such are the rich,
That have abundance and enjoy it not.
King—2 Henry IV IV.iv

Fortune is painted blind, with a muffler afore her eyes, to
signify to you that Fortune is blind; and she is painted also
with a wheel, to signify to you, which is the moral of it, that
she is turning, and inconstant, and mutability, and varia-

tion; and her foot, look you, is fixed upon a spherical stone, which rolls, and rolls, and rolls: in good truth, the poet makes a most excellent description of it: Fortune is an excellent moral.   *Fluellen—Henry V III.vi*

Men at some time are masters of their fates:
The fault, dear Brutus, is not in our stars,
But in ourselves, that we are underlings.   *Cassius—JC I.ii*

Out, out, thou strumpet Fortune! All you gods,
In general synod, take away her power;
Break all the spokes and fellies from her wheel,
And bowl the round nave down the hill of heaven,
As low as to the fiends!   *First Player—Hamlet II.ii*

Who can control his fate?
Othello—Othello V.ii

A good man's fortune may grow out at heels.
Kent—Lear II.ii

Fortune, good night: smile once more; turn thy wheel!
Kent—Lear II.ii

When Fortune in her shift and change of mood
Spurns down her late beloved, all his dependants
Which labour'd after him to the mountain's top
Even on their knees and hands, let him slip down,
Not one accompanying his declining foot.   *Poet—Timon I.i*

Fortune knows
We scorn her most when most she offers blows.
Antony—A&C III.xi

Fortune brings in some boats that are not steer'd.
Pisanio—Cymbeline IV.iii

FRIENDSHIP: "The heart of brothers"

Thou common friend, that's without faith or love,
For such is a friend now; treacherous man!
Thou hast beguiled my hopes; nought but mine eye
Could have persuaded me: now I dare not say
I have one friend alive; thou wouldst disprove me.
Valentine—TGV V.iv

We grew together,
Like to a double cherry, seeming parted,
But yet an union in partition;
Two lovely berries moulded on one stem;
So, with two seeming bodies, but one heart;
Due but to one and crowned with one crest.
And will you rent our ancient love asunder,
To join with men in scorning your poor friend?
It is not friendly, 'tis not maidenly:
Our sex, as well as I, may chide you for it,
Though I alone do feel the injury.   *Helena—MND III.ii*

When to the sessions of sweet silent thought
I summon up remembrance of things past,
I sigh the lack of many a thing I sought,
And with old woes new wail my dear time's waste:
Then can I drown an eye (unused to flow)
For precious friends hid in death's dateless night,
And weep afresh love's long since cancelled woe,
And moan th' expense of many a vanished sight.
Then can I grieve at grievances foregone,

And heavily from woe to woe tell o'er
The sad account of fore-bemoaned moan,
Which I new pay as if not paid before.
>   But if the while I think on thee (dear friend)
>   All losses are restored, and sorrows end.   *Sonnet 30*

If thou wilt lend this money, lend it not
As to thy friends; for when did friendship take
A breed for barren metal of his friend?   *Antonio—MV I.iii*

>   In companions
That do converse and waste the time together,
Whose souls do bear an equal yoke of love,
There must be needs a like proportion
Of lineaments, of manners and of spirit.   *Portia—MV III.iv*

I count myself in nothing else so happy
As in a soul rememb'ring my good friends;
And, as my fortune ripens with thy love,
It shall be still thy true love's recompense.
>   *Bolingbroke—Richard II II.iii*

By God, I cannot flatter; I do defy
The tongues of soothers; but a braver place
In my heart's love hath no man than yourself.
>   *Hotspur—1 Henry IV IV.i*

>   A friend i' the court is better than a penny in purse.
>   *Justice Shallow—2 Henry IV V.i*

I have not from your eyes that gentleness
And show of love as I was wont to have:
You bear too stubborn and too strange a hand
Over your friend that loves you.   *Cassius—JC I.ii*

Friends, Romans, countrymen, lend me your ears;
I come to bury Caesar, not to praise him.
The evil that men do lives after them;
The good is oft interred with their bones;
So let it be with Caesar. The noble Brutus
Hath told you Caesar was ambitious;
If it were so, it was a grievous fault,
And grievously hath Caesar answer'd it.
Here, under leave of Brutus and the rest—
For Brutus is an honourable man;
So are they all, all honourable men—
Come I to speak in Caesar's funeral.
He was my friend, faithful and just to me:
But Brutus says he was ambitious;
And Brutus is an honourable man.
He hath brought many captives home to Rome,
Whose ransoms did the general coffers fill:
Did this in Caesar seem ambitious?
When that the poor have cried, Caesar hath wept.
Ambition should be made of sterner stuff:
Yet Brutus says he was ambitious;
And Brutus is an honourable man.
You all did see that on the Lupercal
I thrice presented him a kingly crown,
Which he did thrice refuse; was this ambition?
Yet Brutus says he was ambitious;
And, sure, he is an honourable man.
I speak not to disprove what Brutus spoke,
But here I am to speak what I do know.
You all did love him once, not without cause:
What cause withholds you then, to mourn for him?
O judgement! thou art fled to brutish beasts,
And men have lost their reason. Bear with me;
My heart is in the coffin there with Caesar,
And I must pause till it come back to me.

Antony—JC III.ii

A friend should bear his friend's infirmities.

Cassius—JC IV.iii

Since my dear soul was mistress of her choice
And could of men distinguish her election,
S' hath seal'd thee for herself; for thou hast been
As one, in suff'ring all, that suffers nothing,
A man that fortune's buffets and rewards
Hast ta'en with equal thanks: and blest are those
Whose blood and judgement are so well commeddled,
That they are not a pipe for fortune's finger
To sound what stop she please. Give me that man
That is not passion's slave, and I will wear him
In my heart's core, ay, in my heart of heart,
As I do thee. *Hamlet—Hamlet III.ii*

Ceremony was but devis'd at first
To set a gloss on faint deeds, hollow welcomes,
Recanting goodness, sorry ere 'tis shown;
But where there is true friendship, there needs none.

Timon—Timon I.ii

O you gods, think I, what need we have any friends, if we should ne'er have need of 'em? they were the most needless creatures living, should we ne'er have use for 'em, and would most resemble sweet instruments hung up in cases that keeps their sounds to themselves. *Timon—Timon I.ii*

Happier is he that has no friend to feed
Than such that do e'en enemies exceed.

Flavius—Timon I.ii

Let molten coin be thy damnation,
Thou disease of a friend, and not himself!

Has friendship such a faint and milky heart,
It turns in less than two nights?   *Flaminius—Timon III.i*

          Let me have thy hand:
Further this act of grace; and from this hour
The heart of brothers govern in our loves
And sway our great designs!   *Antony—A&C II.ii*

O world, thy slippery turns! Friends now fast sworn,
Whose double bosoms seems to wear one heart,
Whose hours, whose bed, whose meal, and exercise,
Are still together, who twin, as 'twere, in love
Unseparable, shall within this hour,
On a dissension of a doit, break out
To bitterest enmity: so, fellest foes,
Whose passions and whose plots have broke their sleep
To take the one the other, by some chance,
Some trick now worth an egg, shall grow dear friends
And interjoin their issues.   *Coriolanus—Coriolanus IV.iv*

The general is my lover: I have been
The book of his good acts, whence men have read
His fame unparallel'd, haply amplified;
For I have ever verified my friends,
Of whom he's chief, with all the size that verity
Would without lapsing suffer.   *Menenius—Coriolanus V.ii*

          And here being thus together,
We are an endless mine to one another;
We are one another's wife, ever begetting
New births of love; we are father, friends, acquaintance,
We are, in one another, families;
I am your heir and you are mine.   *Arcite—TNK II.ii*
.

G

GOVERNMENT: "The specialty of rule"

Civil dissension is a viperous worm
That gnaws the bowels of the commonwealth.

King—1 Henry VI III.i

The presence of a king engenders love
Amongst his subjects and his loyal friends,
As it disanimates his enemies.   *Gloucester—1 Henry VI III.i*

Tis much when sceptres are in children's hands;
But more when envy breeds division;
There comes the ruin, there begins confusion.

Exeter—1 Henry VI IV.i

Woe to that land that's govern'd by a child!

Third Citizen—Richard III II.iii

Go, bind up yon dangling apricocks,
Which, like unruly children, make their sire
Stoop with oppression of their prodigal weight:
Give some supportance to the bending twigs.
Go thou, and like an executioner,
Cut off the heads of too fast growing sprays
That look too lofty in our commonwealth:
All must be even in our government.

Gardener—Richard II III.iv

> We at time of year
> Do wound the bark, the skin of our fruit-trees,
> Lest, being over-proud in sap and blood,
> With too much riches it confound itself:
> Had he done so to great and growing men,
> They might have liv'd to bear and he to taste
> Their fruits of duty: superfluous branches
> We lop away, that bearing boughs may live:
> Had he done so, himself had borne the crown,
> Which waste of idle hours hath quite thrown down.
>
> *Gardener—Richard II III.iv*

> When lenity and cruelty play for a kingdom,
> The gentler gamester is the soonest winner.
>
> *King Henry—Henry V III.vi*

> Whether it be the fault and glimpse of newness,
> Or whether that the body public be
> A horse whereon the governor doth ride,
> Who, newly in the seat, that it may know
> He can command, lets it straight feel the spur;
> Whether the tyranny be in his place,
> Or in his eminence that fills it up,
> I stagger in.
>
> *Claudio—MforM I.ii*

> O, when degree is shak'd,
> Which is the ladder to all high designs,
> The enterprise is sick! How could communities,
> Degrees in schools and brotherhoods in cities,
> Peaceful commerce from dividable shores,
> The primogenity and due of birth,
> Prerogative of age, crowns, scepters, laurels,
> But by degree, stand in authentic place?

Take but degree away, untune that string,
And, hark, what discord follows!   *Ulysses—TC I.iii*

This bodes some strange eruption to our state.
                              Horatio—Hamlet I.i

Something is rotten in the state of Denmark.
                          Marcellus—Hamlet I.iv

                    The cess of majesty
Dies not alone; but, like a gulf, doth draw
What's near it with it: it is a massy wheel,
Fix'd on the summit of the highest mount,
To whose huge spokes ten thousand lesser things
Are mortis'd and adjoin'd; which, when it falls,
Each small annexment, petty consequence,
Attends the boist'rous ruin. Never alone
Did the king sigh, but with a general groan.
                      Rosencrantz—Hamlet III.iii

                  'Tis the curse of service.
Preferment goes by letter and affection,
And not by old gradation, where each second
Stood heir to th' first.   *Iago—Othello I.i*

We cannot all be masters, nor all masters
Cannot be truly follow'd.   *Iago—Othello I.i*

                    He that depends
Upon your favours swims with fins of lead
And hews down oaks with rushes.
                  Coriolanus—Coriolanus I.i

Faith, there have been many great men that have flattered
the people, who ne'er loved them; and there be many that
they have loved, they know not wherefore: so that, if they
love they know not why, they hate upon no better a ground.

Second Officer—Coriolanus II.ii

'Tis time to fear when tyrants seem to kiss.

Pericles—Pericles I.ii

I' th' commonwealth I would by contraries
Execute all things; for no kind of traffic
Would I admit; no name of magistrate;
Letters should not be known; riches, poverty,
And use of service, none; contract, succession,
Bourn, bound of land, tilth, vineyard, none;
No use of metal, corn, or wine, or oil;
No occupation; all men idle, all;
And women too, but innocent and pure;
No sovereignty.   *Gonzalo—Tempest II.i*

All things in common nature should produce
Without sweat or endeavour: treason, felony,
Sword, pike, knife, gun, or need of any engine,
Would I not have, but nature should bring forth,
Of its own kind, all foison, all abundance,
To feed my innocent people.   *Gonzalo—Tempest II.i*

GRIEF: "Give sorrow words"

Honest plain words best pierce the ear of grief.

Berowne—LLL V.ii

Mirth cannot move a soul in agony.
Berowne—LLL V.ii

Oft have I heard that grief softens the mind
And makes it fearful and degenerate.
Queen—2 Henry VI IV.iv

I will instruct my sorrows to be proud;
For grief is proud and makes his owner stoop.
Constance—King John III.i

Grief fills the room up of my absent child,
Lies on his bed, walks up and down with me,
Puts on his pretty looks, repeats his words,
Remembers me of all his gracious parts,
Stuffs out his vacant garments with his form.
Constance—King John III.iv

Sorrow concealed, like an oven stopp'd,
Doth burn the heart to cinders where it is.
Marcus—Titus II.iv

Well, every one can master a grief but he that has it.
Benedick—Much Ado III.ii

Joy absent, grief is present for that time.
Bolingbroke—Richard II I.iii

Each substance of a grief hath twenty shadows,
Which shows like grief itself, but is not so;
For sorrow's eye, blazed with blinding tears,
Divides one thing entire to many objects;
Like perspectives, which rightly gaz'd upon

Show nothing but confusion, ey'd awry
Distinguish form.   *Bushy—Richard II II.ii*

Now hath my soul brought forth her prodigy,
And I, a gasping new-deliver'd mother,
Have woe to woe, sorrow to sorrow join'd.
                             Queen—Richard II II.ii

Moderate lamentation is the right of the dead, excessive
grief the enemy to the living.   *Countess—All's Well I.i*

But sorrow, that is couch'd in seeming gladness,
Is like that mirth fate turns to sudden sadness.
                                    Troilus—TC I.i

When sorrows come, they come not single spies,
But in battalions.   *Claudius—Hamlet IV.v*

              From this instant,
There's nothing serious in mortality;
All is but toys; renown and grace is dead;
The wine of life is drawn, and the mere lees
Is left this vault to brag of.   *Macbeth—Macbeth II.iii*

To show an unfelt sorrow is an office
Which the false man does easy.   *Malcolm—Macbeth II.iii*

Give sorrow words: the grief that does not speak
Whispers the o'er fraught heart and bids it break.
                                    Malcolm—Macbeth IV.iii

This grief is crowned with consolation; your old smock
brings forth a new petticoat: and indeed the tears live in an
onion that should water this sorrow.   *Enobarbus—A&C I.ii*

All strange and terrible events are welcome,
But comforts we despise; our size of sorrow,
Proportion'd to our cause, must be as great
As that which makes it.   *Cleopatra—A&C IV.xv*

One sorrow never comes but brings an heir,
That may succeed as his inheritor.   *Cleon—Pericles I.iv*

      What's gone and what's past help
Should be past grief.   *Paulina—WT III.ii*

H

HONOUR: "Far more precious-dear than life"

Undaunted spirit in a dying breast!
Talbot—1 Henry VI III.ii

A heart unspotted is not easily daunted.
Gloucester—2 Henry VI III.i

True nobility is exempt from fear.
Suffolk—2 Henry VI IV.i

What valour were it, when a cur doth grin,
For one to thrust his hand between his teeth,
When he might spurn him with his foot away?
Northumberland—3 Henry VI I.iv

Sweet mercy is nobility's true badge.
Tamora—Titus I.i

In a false quarrel there is no true valour.
Benedick—Much Ado V.i

Mine honour is my life; both grow in one;
Take honour from me, and my life is done.
Mowbray—Richard II I.i

That which in mean men we intitle patience
Is pale cold cowardice in noble breasts.

Duchess—Richard II I.ii

By heaven, methinks it were an easy leap,
To pluck bright honour from the pale-fac'd moon,
Or dive into the bottom of the deep,
Where fathom-line could never touch the ground,
And pluck up drowned honour by the locks;
So he that doth redeem her thence might wear
Without corrival all her dignities:

Hotspur—1 Henry IV I.iii

Well, 'tis no matter; honour pricks me on. Yea, but how if
honour prick me off when I come on? how then? Can honour set to a leg? no: or an arm? no: or take away the grief of
a wound? no. Honour hath no skill in surgery, then? no.
What is honour? a word. What is in that word honour?
what is that honour? air. A trim reckoning! Who hath it? he
that died a Wednesday. Doth he feel it? no. Doth he hear it?
no. 'Tis insensible, then? Yea, to the dead. But will it not live
with the living? no. Why? detraction will not suffer it.
Therefore I'll none of it. Honour is a mere scutcheon: and so
ends my catechism.

Falstaff—1 Henry IV V.i

Give me life: which if I can save, so; if not, honour comes
unlooked for, and there's an end.   *Falstaff—1 Henry IV V.iii*

Virtue is of so little regard in these costermongers' times
that true valour is turned bearherd. *Falstaff—2 Henry IV I.ii*

Now all the youth of England are on fire,
And silken dalliance in the wardrobe lies:
Now thrive the armourers, and honour's thought

Reigns solely in the breast of every man.
They sell the pasture now to buy the horse,
Following the mirror of all Christian kings,
With winged heels, as English Mercuries.

Chorus—Henry V II.Prologue

If we are mark'd to die, we are enow
To do our country loss; and if to live,
The fewer men, the greater share of honour.

King Henry—Henry V IV.iii

Methinks I could not die any where so contented as in the
king's company; his cause being just and his quarrel honourable.   *Henry—Henry V IV.i*

If it be aught toward the general good,
Set honour in one eye and death i' the other,
And I will look on both indifferently:
For let the gods so speed me as I love
The name of honour more than I fear death.

Cassius—JC I ii

                    See that you come
Not to woo honour, but to wed it; when
The bravest questant shrinks, find what you seek,
That fame may cry you loud.   *King—All's Well II.i*

                    Honours thrive,
When rather from our acts we them derive
Than our foregoers: the mere word's a slave
Debosh'd on every tomb, on every grave
A lying trophy, and as oft is dumb
Where dust and damn'd oblivion is the tomb
Of honour'd bones indeed.   *King—All's Well II.iii*

He wears his honour in a box unseen,
That hugs his kicky-wicky here at home,
Spending his manly marrow in her arms,
Which should sustain the bound and high curvet
Of Mars's fiery steed.   *Parolles—All's Well II.iii*

Mine honour keeps the weather of my fate:
Life every man holds dear; but the dear man
Holds honour far more precious-dear than life.
                                          Hector—TC V.iii

                    Rightly to be great
Is not to stir without great argument,
But greatly to find quarrel in a straw
When honour's at the stake.   *Hamlet—Hamlet IV.iv*

                    Thou must know,
'Tis not my profit that does lead mine honour;
Mine honour, it.   *Pompey—A&C II.vii*

                    If I lose mine honour,
I lose myself.   *Antony—A&C III.iv*

I would dissemble with my nature where
My fortunes and my friends at stake requir'd
I should do so in honour.   *Volumnia—Coriolanus III.ii*

                    Honour we love;
For who hates honour hates the gods above.
                                    Simonides—Pericles II.iii

If you were born to honour, show it now;
If put upon you, make the judgement good
That thought you worthy of it.   *Marina—Pericles IV.vi*

He sits 'mongst men like a descended god;
He hath a kind of honour sets him off,
More than a mortal seeming.   *Iachimo—Cymbeline I.vi*

For life, I prize it
As I weigh grief, which I would spare: for honour,
'Tis a derivative from me to mine,
And only that I stand for.   *Hermione—WT III.ii*

Honour's train
Is longer than his foreskirt.   *Old Lady—Henry VIII II.iii*

HOSPITALITY: "Good digestion wait on appetite"

Small cheer and great welcome makes a merry feast.
        Balthasar—CE III.i

A man is never undone till he be hanged, nor never welcome to a place till some certain shot be paid and the hostess say "Welcome!"   *Launce—TGV II.v*

Unbidden guests
Are often welcomest when they are gone.
        Bedford—1 Henry VI II.ii

I hope we shall all drink down unkindness.
        Page—Merry Wives I.i

To the latter end of a fray and the beginning of a feast,
Fits a dull fighter and a keen guest.
        Falstaff—1 Henry IV IV.ii

I wonder men dare trust themselves with men:
Methinks they should invite them without knives;
Good for their meat, and safer for their lives.

Apemantus—Timon I.ii

The west yet glimmers with some streaks of day.
Now spurs the lated traveller apace
To gain the timely inn. *First Murderer—Macbeth III.iii*

The feast is sold
That is not often vouch'd, while 'tis a-making,
'Tis given with welcome: to feed were best at home;
From thence the sauce to meat is ceremony;
Meeting were bare without it.

Lady Macbeth—Macbeth III.iv

Now, good digestion wait on appetite,
And health on both! *Macbeth—Macbeth III.iv*

Come, let's all take hands,
Till that the conquering wine hath steep'd our sense
In soft and delicate Lethe. *Antony—A&C II.vii*

Come, thou monarch of the vine,
Plumpy Bacchus with pink eyne!
In thy fats our cares be drown'd,
With thy grapes our hairs be crown'd:
Cup us, till the world go round,
Cup us, till the world go round! *Enobarbus—A&C II.vii*

I

ILLNESS: "We are all diseas'd"

As fest'red members rot but by degree,
Till bones and flesh and sinews fall away,
So will this base and envious discord breed.

Exeter—1 Henry VI III.i

For to strange sores strangely they strain the cure.

Friar—Much Ado IV.i

For my belly's as cold as if I had swallowed snowballs for
pills to cool the reins.   *Falstaff—Merry Wives III.v*

Deep malice makes too deep incision;
Forget, forgive; conclude and be agreed;
Our doctors say this is no month to bleed.

King Richard—Richard II I.i

Sick now! droop now! this sickness doth infect
The very life-blood of our enterprise.

Hotspur—1 Henry IV IV.i

A pox of this gout! or a gout of this pox! for the one or the
other plays the rogue with my great toe.

Falstaff—2 Henry IV I.ii

A good wit will make use of any thing: I will turn
diseases to commodity. *Falstaff—2 Henry IV I.ii*

We are all diseas'd,
And with our surfeiting and wanton hours,
Have brought ourselves into a burning fever,
And we must bleed for it. *Archbishop—2 Henry IV IV.i*

Against ill chances men are ever merry;
But heaviness foreruns the good event.
Archbishop—2 Henry IV IV.ii

He hath the falling-sickness.
Brutus—JC I.ii

So play the foolish throngs with one that swoons;
Come all to help him, and so stop the air
By which he should revive. *Angelo—MforM II.iv*

Diseases desperate grown
By desperate appliance are reliev'd,
Or not at all. *Claudius—Hamlet IV.iii*

Infirmity doth still neglect all office
Whereto our health is bound; we are not ourselves
When nature, being oppress'd, commands the mind
To suffer with the body. *Lear—Lear II.iv*

Canst thou not minister to a mind diseas'd,
Pluck from the memory a rooted sorrow,
Raze out the written troubles of the brain
And with some sweet oblivious antidote
Cleanse the stuff'd bosom of that perilous stuff
Which weighs upon the heart? *Macbeth—Macbeth V.iii*

                    The service of the foot
Being once gangren'd, is not then respected
For what before it was.   *Menenius—Coriolanus III.i*

He was not taken well; he had not din'd;
The veins unfill'd, our blood is cold, and then
We pout upon the morning, are unapt
To give or to forgive; but when we have stuff'd
These pipes and these conveyances of our blood
With wine and feeding, we have suppler souls
Than in our priest-like fasts.   *Menenius—Coriolanus V.i*

J

JUSTICE AND LAW: "The quality of mercy is not strain'd"

Between two hawks, which flies the higher pitch;
Between two blades, which bears the better temper;
Between two dogs, which hath the deeper mouth;
Between two horses, which doth bear him best;
Between two girls, which hath the merriest eye;
I have perhaps some shallow spirit of judgement;
But in these nice sharp quillets of the law,
Good faith, I am no wiser than a daw.

Warwick—1 Henry VI II.iv

Thrice is he arm'd that hath his quarrel just,
And he but naked, though lock'd up in steel,
Whose conscience with injustice is corrupted.

King—2 Henry VI III.ii

When law can do no right,
Let it be lawful that law bar no wrong.

Constance—King John III.i

Mercy but murders, pardoning those that kill.

Prince—RJ III.i

The quality of mercy is not strain'd,
It droppeth as the gentle rain from heaven
Upon the place beneath: it is twice blest;

It blesseth him that gives and him that takes:
'Tis mightiest in the mightiest: it becomes
The throned monarch better than his crown;
His sceptre shows the force of temporal power,
The attribute to awe and majesty,
Wherein doth sit the dread and fear of kings;
But mercy is above this sceptred sway;
It is enthroned in the hearts of kings,
It is an attribute to God himself;
And earthly power doth then show likest God's
When mercy seasons justice.   *Portia—MV IV.i*

Shall there be gallows standing in England when thou art
king? and resolution thus fubbed as it is with the rusty curb
of old father antic the law?   *Falstaff—1 Henry IV I.ii*

So shall I live to speak my father's words:
'Happy am I, that have a man so bold,
That dares do justice on my proper son:
And not less happy, having such a son,
That would deliver up his greatness so
Into the hands of justice.'   *King Henry V—2 Henry IV V.ii*

If little faults, proceeding on distemper,
Shall not be wink'd at, how shall we stretch our eye
When capital crimes, chew'd, swallow'd and digested,
Appear before us?   *King Henry—Henry V II.ii*

Thus can the demigod Authority
Make us pay down for our offence by weight
The words of heaven; on whom it will, it will:
On whom it will not, so; yet still 'tis just.
          Claudio—MforM I.ii

We must not make a scarecrow of the law,
Setting it up to fear the birds of prey
And let it keep one shape, till custom make it
Their perch and not their terror.   *Angelo—MforM II.i*

                    I not deny,
The jury, passing on the prisoner's life,
May in the sworn twelve have a thief or two
Guiltier than him they try. What's open made to justice,
That justice seizes: what knows the laws
That thieves do pass on thieves?   *Angelo—MforM II.i*

Mercy is not itself, that oft looks so;
Pardon is still the nurse of second woe.
                              Escalus—MforM II.i

                    I have seen,
When, after execution, judgement hath
Repented o'er his doom.   *Provost—MforM II.ii*

No ceremony that to great ones 'longs,
Not the king's crowns, nor the deputed sword,
The marshal's truncheon, nor the judge's robe,
Become them with one half so good a grace
As mercy does.   *Isabella—MforM II.ii*

                But man, proud man,
Drest in a little brief authority,
Most ignorant of what he's most assur'd,
His glassy essence, like an angry ape,
Plays such fantastic tricks before high heaven
As makes the angels weep; who, with our spleens,
Would all themselves laugh mortal.   *Isabella—MforM II.ii*

Thieves for their robbery have authority
When judges steal themselves.   *Angelo—MforM II.ii*

Ignomy in ransom and free pardon
Are of two houses: lawful mercy
Is nothing kin to foul redemption.   *Isabella—MforM II.iv*

                    O perilous mouths,
That bear in them one and the self-same tongue,
Either of condemnation or approof;
Bidding the law make court'sy to their will;
Hooking both right and wrong to th' appetite,
To follow as it draws!   *Isabella—MforM II.iv*

He who the sword of heaven will bear
Should be as holy as severe;
Pattern in himself to know,
Grace to stand, and virtue go;
More nor less to others paying
Than by self-offences weighing.
Shame to him whose cruel striking
Kills for faults of his own liking!   *Duke—MforM III.ii*

When vice makes mercy, mercy's so extended,
That for the fault's love is th' offender friended.
                          Duke—MforM IV.ii

O, be persuaded! do not count it holy
To hurt by being just: it is as lawful,
For we would give much, to use violent thefts,
And rob in the behalf of charity.   *Andromache—TC V.iii*

Let the superfluous and lust-dieted man,
That slaves your ordinance, that will not see

Because he does not feel, feel your pow'r quickly;
So distribution should undo excess,
And each man have enough. *Gloucester—Lear IV.i*

Through tatter'd clothes small vices do appear;
Robes and furr'd gowns hide all. Plate sin with gold,
And the strong lance of justice hurtless breaks;
Arm it in rags, a pigmy's straw does pierce it.
Lear—Lear IV.vi

The gods are just, and of our pleasant vices
Make instruments to plague us. *Edgar—Lear V.iii*

Nothing emboldens sin so much as mercy.
First Senator—Timon III.v

For pity is the virtue of the law,
And none but tyrants use it cruelly. *Alcibiades—Timon III.v*

If the great gods be just, they shall assist
The deeds of justest men. *Pompey—A&C II.i*

You wear out a good wholesome forenoon in hearing a
cause between an orange-wife and a forset-seller; and then
rejourn the controversy of three pence to a second day of
audience. When you are hearing a matter between party
and party, if you chance to be pinched with the colic, you
make faces like mummers; set up the bloody flag against all
patience; and, in roaring for a chamber-pot, dismiss the
controversy bleeding, the more entangled by your hearing;
all the peace you make in their cause is, calling both the parties knaves. *Menenius—Coriolanus II.i*

L

LOVE: "What is love?"

Love is a familiar; Love is a devil: there is no evil angel but
Love.   *Armado—LLL I.ii*

But love, first learned in a lady's eyes,
Lives not alone immured in the brain;
But, with the motion of all elements,
Courses as swift as thought in every power,
And gives to every power a double power,
Above their functions and their offices.
It adds a precious seeing to the eye;
A lover's eyes will gaze an eagle blind;
A lover's ear will hear the lowest sound,
When the suspicious head of theft is stopp'd:
Love's feeling is more soft and sensible
Than are the tender horns of cockled snails;
Love's tongue proves dainty Bacchus gross in taste:
For valour, is not Love a Hercules,
Still climbing trees in the Hesperides?
Subtle as Sphinx; as sweet and musical
As bright Apollo's lute, strung with his hair;
And when Love speaks, the voice of all the gods
Make heaven drowsy with the harmony.
Never durst poet touch a pen to write
Until his ink were temp'red with Love's sighs;
O, then his lines would ravish savage ears

And plant in tyrants mild humility.
From woman's eyes this doctrine I derive;
They sparkle still the right Promethean fire;
They are the books, the arts, the academes,
That show, contain and nourish all the world:
Else none at all in aught proves excellent.

Berone—LLL IV.iii

Love is your master, for he masters you.

Valentine—TGV I.i

They do not love that do not show their love.

Julia—TGV I.ii

Fie, fie, how wayward is this foolish love,
That like a testy babe will scratch the nurse
And presently, all humbled, kiss the rod.   *Julia—TGV I.ii*

He, being in love, could not see to garter his hose, and you,
being in love, cannot see to put on your hose.

Speed—TGV II.i

If she do frown, 'tis not in hate of you,
But rather to beget more love in you;
If she do chide, 'tis not to have you gone;
For why, the fools are mad, if left alone.
Take no repulse, whatever she doth say;
For 'get you gone,' she doth not mean 'away!'
Flatter and praise, commend, extol their graces;
Though ne'er so black, say they have angels' faces.
That man that hath a tongue, I say, is no man,
If with his tongue he cannot win a woman.

Valentine—TGV III.i

Hope is a lover's staff; walk hence with that
And manage it against despairing thoughts.

Proteus—TGV III.i

Alas, how love can trifle with itself!

Julia—TGV IV.iv

O, 'tis the curse in love, and still approved,
When women cannot love where they're beloved!

Proteus—TGV V.iv

The course of true love never did run smooth.

Lysander—MND I.i

Things base and vile, holding no quantity,
Love can transpose to form and dignity;
Love looks not with the eyes, but with the mind;
And therefore is wing'd Cupid painted blind;
Nor hath Love's mind of any judgement taste;
Wings and no eyes figure unheedy haste:
And therefore is Love said to be a child,
Because in choice he is so oft beguil'd.
As waggish boys in game themselves forswear,
So the boy Love is perjur'd everywhere.   *Helena—MND I.i*

Lovers and madmen have such seething brains,
Such shaping fantasies, that apprehend
More than cool reason ever comprehends.
The lunatic, the lover and the poet
Are of imagination all compact;
One sees more devils than vast hell can hold,
That is, the madman: the lover, all as frantic,
Sees Helen's beauty in a brow of Egypt:
The poet's eye, in a fine frenzy rolling,

Doth glance from heaven to earth, from earth to heaven;
And as imagination bodies forth
The forms of things unknown, the poet's pen
Turns them to shapes and gives to airy nothing
A local habitation and a name.
Such tricks hath strong imagination,
That, if it would apprehend some joy
It comprehends some bringer of that joy;
Or, in the night, imagining some fear,
How easy is a bush suppos'd a bear!   *Theseus—MND V.i*

Alas, that love, so gentle in his view,
Should be so tyrannous and rough in proof!   *Benvolio—RJ I.i*

Love is a smoke rais'd with the fume of sighs;
Being purg'd, a fire sparkling in lovers' eyes;
Being vex'd, a sea nourish'd with lovers' tears;
What is it else? a madness most discreet,
A choking gall and a preserving sweet.   *Romeo—RJ I.i*

This precious book of love, this unbound lover,
To beautify him, only lacks a cover: *Lady Capulet—RJ I.iii*

Is love a tender thing? it is too rough,
Too rude, too boist'rous, and it pricks like thorn
Romeo—RJ I.iv

This bud of love, by summer's ripening breath,
May prove a beauteous flow'r when next we meet
Juliet—RJ II.ii

Love goes toward love, as schoolboys from their books,
But love from love, toward school with heavy looks.
Romeo—RJ II.ii

How silver-sweet sound lovers' tongues by night,
Like softest music to attending ears!   *Romeo— RJ II.ii*

This drivelling love is like a great natural, that runs lolling
up and down to hide his bauble in a hole.
Mercutio—RJ II.iv

Love's heralds should be thoughts,
Which ten times faster glide than the sun's beams,
Driving back shadows over louring hills:
Therefore do nimble-pinion'd doves draw love,
And therefore hath the wind-swift Cupid wings.
Juliet—RJ II.v

The sweetest honey
Is loathsome in his own deliciousness
And in the taste confounds the appetite:
Therefore love moderately: long love doth so;
Too swift arrives as tardy as too slow.
Friar Laurence—RJ II.vi

Venus smiles not in a house of tears.
Paris—RJ IV.i

Love comforteth like sunshine after rain,
But Lust's effect is tempest after sun;
Love's gentle spring doth always fresh remain,
Lust's winter comes ere summer half be done;
Love surfeits not, Lust like a glutton dies;
Love is all truth, Lust full of forged lies.
Venus—V&A 799–804

But love is blind and lovers cannot see
The pretty follies that themselves commit.

Jessica—MV II.vi

Tell me, where is fancy bred,
Or in the heart or in the head?
How begot, how nourished?
Reply, reply.
It is engend'red in the eyes,
With gazing fed; and fancy dies
In the cradle where it lies.
Let us all ring fancy's knell;
I'll begin it—Ding, dong, bell.
Ding, dong, bell.

MV III.ii

Speak low, if you speak love.

Don Pedro—Much Ado II.i

Friendship is constant in all other things
Save in the office and affairs of love;
Therefore all hearts in love use their own tongues;
Let every eye negotiate for itself
And trust no agent; for beauty is a witch
Against whose charms faith melteth into blood.

Claudio—Much Ado II.i

Sigh no more, ladies, sigh no more,
Men were deceivers ever,
One foot in sea and one on shore,
To one thing constant never:
Then sigh not so, but let them go,
And be you blithe and bonny,
Converting all your sounds of woe
Into Hey, nonny, nonny. *Balthasar—Much Ado II.iii*

Then loving goes by haps:
Some Cupid kills with arrows, some with traps.

Hero—Much Ado III.i

Love like a shadow flies when substance love pursues;
Pursuing that that flies, and flying what pursues.

Ford—Merry Wives II.ii

O powerful love! that, in some respects, makes a beast a
man, in some other, a man a beast! You were also, Jupiter, a
swan for the love of Leda. O omnipotent Love! How near
the god drew to the complexion of a goose! A fault done
first in the form of a beast. O Jove, a beastly fault! And then
another fault in the semblance of a fowl; think on't Jove, a
foul fault! When gods have hot backs, what shall poor men
do?   *Falstaff—Merry Wives V.v*

In love the heavens themselves do guide the state;
Money buys lands, and wives are sold by fate.

Ford—Merry Wives V.v

If thou rememb'rest not the slightest folly
That ever love did make thee run into,
Thou hast not lov'd.   *Silvius—AYLI II.iv*

We that are true lovers run into strange capers; but as all is
mortal in nature, so is all nature in love mortal in folly.

Touchstone—AYLI II.iv

Love is merely a madness, and, I tell you, deserves as well a
dark house and a whip as madmen do: and the reason why
they are not so punished and cured is, that the lunacy is so
ordinary that the whippers are in love too.

Rosalind—AYLI III.ii

The poor world is almost six thousand years old, and in all this time there was not any man died in his own person, videlicet, in a love cause. Troilus had his brains dashed out with a Grecian club; yet he did what he could to die before, and he is one of the patterns of love. Leander, he would have lived many a fair year, though Hero had turned nun, if it had not been for a hot mid-summer night; for, good youth, he went but forth to wash him in the Hellespont and being taken with the cramp was drowned: and the foolish chroniclers of that age found it was 'Hero of Sestos.' But these are all lies: men have died from time to time and worms have eaten them, but not for love.

Rosalind—AYLI IV.i

Wilt thou love such a woman? What, to make thee an instrument and play false strains upon thee! not to be endured! Well, go your way to her, but I see love have made thee a tame snake.

Rosalind—AYLI IV.iii

For your brother and my sister no sooner met but they looked, no sooner looked but they loved, no sooner loved but they sighed, no sooner sighed but they asked one another the reason, no sooner knew the reason but they sought the remedy; and in these degrees have they made a pair of stairs to marriage which they will climb incontinent, or else be incontinent before marriage; they are in the very wrath of love and they will together; clubs cannot part them.

Rosalind—AYLI V.ii

Away before me to sweet beds of flow'rs:
Love-thoughts lie rich when canopied with bow'rs.

Orsino—TN I.i

O mistress mine, where are you roaming?
O, stay and hear; your true love's coming,
 That can sing both high and low:
Trip no further, pretty sweeting;
Journeys end in lovers meeting,
 Every wise man's son doth know.

What is love? 'tis not hereafter;
Present mirth hath present laughter;
 What's to come is still unsure:
In delay there lies no plenty;
Then come to kiss me, sweet and twenty,
 Youth's a stuff will not endure. *Feste—TN II.iii*

A murd'rous guilt shows not itself more soon
Than love that would seem hid: love's night is noon.
         Olivia—TN III.i

 Love sought is good, but given unsought is better.
         Viola—TN III.i

Th' ambition in my love thus plagues itself:
The hind that would be mated by the lion
Must die for love.   *Helena—All's Well I.i*

Believe not that the dribbling dart of love
Can pierce a complete bosom. *Duke—MforM I.iii*

Love, love, nothing but love, still love, still more!
  For, O, love's bow
  Shoots buck and doe:
  The shaft confounds,
  Not that it wounds,
But tickles still the sore.

These lovers cry Oh! oh! they die!
    Yet that which seems the wound to kill,
Doth turn oh! oh! to ha! ha! he!
    So dying love lives still:
Oh! oh! a while, but ha! ha! ha!
Oh! oh! groans out for ha! ha! ha!   *Pandarus—TC III.i*

He eats nothing but doves, love, and that breeds hot blood,
and hot blood begets hot thoughts, and hot thoughts beget
hot deeds, and hot deeds is love.   *Paris—TC III.i*

Is this the generation of love? hot blood, hot thoughts, and
hot deeds? Why, they are vipers; is love a generation of
vipers?   *Pandarus—TC III.i*

This is the very ecstacy of love,
Whose violent property fordoes itself
And leads the will to desperate undertakings
As oft as any passion under heaven
That does afflict our natures.   *Polonius—Hamlet II.i*

     I know love is begun by time;
And that I see, in passages of proof,
Time qualifies the spark and fire of it.
There lives within the very flame of love
A kind of wick or snuff that will abate it.
     Claudius—Hamlet IV.vii

    There's beggary in the love that can be reckon'd.
     Antony—A&C I.i

Love's counselor should fill the bores of hearing,
To th' smothering of the sense.   *Imogen—Cymbeline III.ii*

Prosperity's the very bond of love,
Whose fresh complexion and whose heart together
Affliction alters.   *Camillo—WT IV.iv*

                              Oh, Love,
What a stout-hearted child thou art!
                              Daughter—TNK II.vi

LOVE OF COUNTRY: "This precious stone set in the silver sea"

                    Sweet soil, adieu;
My mother, and my nurse, that bears me yet!
Where'er I wander, boast of this I can,
Though banish'd, yet a trueborn Englishman.
                         Bolingbroke—Richard II I.iii

This royal throne of kings, this scept'red isle,
This earth of majesty, this seat of Mars,
This other Eden, demi-paradise,
This fortress built by Nature for herself
Against infection and the hand of war,
This happy breed of men, this little world,
This precious stone set in the silver sea,
Which serves it in the office of a wall
Or as a moat defensive to a house,
Against the envy of less happier lands,
This blessed plot, this earth, this realm, this England,
This nurse, this teeming womb of royal kings,
Fear'd by their breed and famous by their birth,
Renowned for their deeds as far from home,
For Christian service and true chivalry,
As is the supulchre in stubborn Jewry

Of the world's ransom, blessed Mary's Son,
This land of such dear souls, this dear dear land,
Dear for her reputation through the world,
Is now leas'd out, I die pronouncing it,
Like to a tenement or pelting farm.

John of Gaunt—Richard II II.i

Dear earth, I do salute thee with my hand,
Though rebels wound thee with their horses' hoofs:
As a long-parted mother with her child
Plays fondly with her tears and smiles in meeting,
So, weeping, smiling, greet I thee, my earth,
And do thee favours with my royal hands.

King Richard—Richard II III.ii

O my poor kingdom, sick with civil blows!
When that my care could not withhold thy riots,
What wilt thou do when riot is thy care?
O, thou wilt be a wilderness again,
Peopled with wolves, thy old inhabitants!

King—2 Henry IV IV.v

Our countrymen
Are men more order'd than when Julius Caesar
Smil'd at their lack of skill, but found their courage
Worthy his frowning at: their discipline,
Now mingled with their courages, will make known
To their approvers they are people such
That mend upon the world.   *Posthumus—Cymbeline II.iv*

Britain's a world ·
By itself; and we will nothing pay
For wearing our own noses.   *Cloten—Cymbeline III.i*

LOVE SPEAKING: "I will love, write, sigh, pray, sue, groan"

What? I love! I sue! I seek a wife!

Berowne—LLL III.i

Well, I will love, write, sigh, pray, sue, groan:
Some men must love my lady and some Joan.

Berowne—LLL III.i

By the Lord, this love is as mad as Ajax: it kills sheep; it kills me, I a sheep: well proved, again o' my side! I will not love: if I do, hang me; i' faith, I will not. O, but her eye,—by this light, but for her eye, I would not love her; yes, for her two eyes. Well, I do nothing in the world but lie, and lie in my throat. By heaven, I do love, and it hath taught me to rhyme and to be melancholy.   *Berowne—LLL IV.iii*

I have done penance for contemning Love,
Whose high imperious thoughts have punish'd me
With bitter fasts, with penitential groans,
With nightly tears and daily heart-sore sighs;
For in revenge of my contempt of love,
Love hath chas'd sleep from my enthralled eyes
And made them watchers of mine own heart's sorrow.

Valentine—TGV II.iv

Love bade me swear, and Love bids me forswear.
O sweet-suggesting Love, if thou hast sinn'd,
Teach me, thy tempted subject, to excuse it!
At first I did adore a twinkling star,
But now I worship a celestial sun.   *Proteus—TGV II.vi*

He lives not now that knows me to be in love; yet I am in love; but a team of horse shall not pluck that from me; nor who 'tis I love; and yet 'tis a woman; but what woman, I will not tell myself; and yet 'tis a milkmaid; yet 'tis not a maid, for she hath had gossips; yet 'tis a maid, for she is her master's maid, and serves for wages. She hath more qualities than a water-spaniel, which is much in a bare Christian.

Launce—TGV III.i

You know that love
Will creep in service where it cannot go.

Proteus—TGV IV.ii

I do desire thee, even from a heart
As full of sorrows as the sea of sands.   *Silvia—TGV IV.iii*

In love, who respects friend?

Proteus—TGV V.iv

I hold him but a fool that will endanger
His body for a girl that loves him not.   *Thurio—TGV V.iv*

For where thou art, there is the world itself,
With every several pleasure in the world,
And where thou art not, desolation.

Suffolk—2 Henry VI III.ii

One fairer than my love! the all-seeing sun
Ne'er saw her match since first the world begun.

Romeo—RJ I.ii

O, she doth teach the torches to burn bright!
It seems she hangs upon the cheek of night

As a rich jewel in an Ethiope's ear;
Beauty too rich for use, for earth too dear!
So shows a snowy dove trooping with crows,
As yonder lady o'er her fellows shows.
The measure done, I'll watch her place of stand,
And, touching hers, make blessed my rude hand.
Did my heart love till now? Forswear it, sight!
For I ne'er saw true beauty till this night.   *Romeo—RJ I.v*

But, soft! what light through yonder window breaks?
It is the east, and Juliet is the sun.
Arise, fair sun, and kill the envious moon,
Who is already sick and pale with grief,
That thou her maid art far more fair than she:
Be not her maid, since she is envious;
Her vestal livery is but sick and green
And none but fools do wear it; cast it off.
It is my lady, O, it is my love!
O, that she knew she were!
She speaks, yet she says nothing: what of that?
Her eye discourses; I will answer it.
I am too bold, 'tis not to me she speaks:
Two of the fairest stars in all the heaven,
Having some business, do entreat her eyes
To twinkle in their spheres till they return.
What if her eyes were there, they in her head?
The brightness of her cheek would shame those stars,
As daylight doth a lamp; her eyes in heaven
Would through the airy region stream so bright
That birds would sing and think it were not night.
See how she leans her cheek upon her hand!
O, that I were a glove upon that hand,
That I might touch that cheek!   *Romeo—RJ II.ii*

My bounty is as boundless as the sea,
My love as deep; the more I give to thee,
The more I have, for both are infinite.   *Juliet—RJ II.ii*

Good night, good night! parting is such sweet sorrow,
That I shall say good night till it be morrow.   *Juliet—RJ II.ii*

              Come, civil night,
Thou sober-suited matron, all in black,—
And learn me how to lose a winning match,
Play'd for a pair of stainless maidenhoods:
Hood my unmann'd blood, bating in my cheeks,
With thy black mantle; till strange love, grown bold,
Think true love acted simple modesty.
Come, night; come, Romeo; come, thou day in night;
For thou wilt lie upon the wings of night
Whiter than new snow upon a raven's back.
Come, gentle night, come, loving, black-brow'd night,
Give me my Romeo; and, when he shall die,
Take him and cut him out in little stars,
And he will make the face of heaven so fine
That all the world will be in love with night
And pay no worship to the garish sun.   *Juliet—RJ III.ii*

My mistress' eyes are nothing like the sun;
Coral is far more red than her lips' red;
If snow be white, why then her breasts are dun;
If hairs be wires, black wires grow on her head.
I have seen roses damask'd, red and white,
But no such roses see I in her cheeks;
And in some perfumes is there more delight
Than in the breath that from my mistress reeks.
I love to hear her speak, yet well I know

That music hath a far more pleasing sound;
I grant I never saw a goddess go;
My mistress when she walks, treads on the ground:
    And yet, by heaven, I think my love as rare
    As any she belied with false compare.   *Sonnet 130*

Beshrew me, but I love her heartily;
For she is wise, if I can judge of her,
And fair she is, if that mine eyes be true,
And true she is, as she hath prov'd herself,
And therefore, like herself, wise, fair and true,
Shall she be placed in my constant soul.   *Lorenzo—MV II.vi*

                For you,
I would be trebled twenty times myself;
A thousand times more fair, ten thousand times
More rich;
That only to stand high in your account,
I might in virtues, beauties, livings, friends,
Exceed account.   *Portia—MV III.ii*

I had rather hear my dog bark at a crow than a man swear
he loves me.   *Beatrice—Much Ado I.i*

Prove that ever I lose more blood with love than I will get
again with drinking, pick out mine eyes with a ballad-maker's
pen and hang me up at the door of a brothel-house for the
sign of blind Cupid.   *Benedick—Much Ado I.i*

I do much wonder that one man, seeing how much another
man is a fool when he dedicates his behaviours to love, will,
after he hath laughed at such shallow follies in others, become the argument of his own scorn by falling in love.
                Benedick—Much Ado II.iii

I will not be sworn but love may transform me to an oyster; but I'll take my oath on it, till he have made an oyster of me, he shall never make me such a fool. One woman is fair, yet I am well; another is wise, yet I am well; another virtuous, yet I am well; but till all graces be in one woman, one woman shall not come in my grace.   *Benedick—Much Ado II.iii*

I cannot cog and say thou art this and that, like a many of these lisping hawthornbuds, that come like women in men's apparel, and smell like Bucklersbury in simple time; I cannot; but I love thee; none but thee; and thou deservest it.
     Falstaff—Merry Wives III.iii

Dead shepherd, now I find thy saw of might,
Who ever lov'd that lov'd not at first sight?
     Phoebe—AYLI III.iv.81-82

Make me a willow cabin at your gate,
And call upon my soul within the house;
Write loyal cantons of contemned love
And sing them loud even in the dead of night.   *Viola—TN I.v*

        If ever thou shalt love,
In the sweet pangs of it remember me;
For such as I am all true lovers are,
Unstaid and skittish in all motions else,
Save in the constant image of the creature
That is belov'd.   *Orsino—TN II.iv*

        There is no woman's sides
Can bide the beating of so strong a passion
As love doth give my heart; no woman's heart
So big, to hold so much; they lack retention.
     Orsino—TN II.iv

She never told her love,
But let concealment, like a worm i' th' bud,
Feed on her damask cheek: she pin'd in thought,
And with a green and yellow melancholy
She sat like Patience on a monument,
Smiling at grief. Was not this love indeed?   *Viola—TN II.iv*

Come, come, in wooing sorrow let's be brief,
Since, wedding it, there is such length in grief:
One kiss shall stop our mouths, and dumbly part;
Thus give I mine, and thus take I thy heart.
King Richard—Richard II V.i

I speak to thee plain soldier: if thou canst love me for this, take me; if not, to say to thee that I shall die, is true; but for thy love, by the Lord, no; yet I love thee too. And while thou livest, dear Kate, take a fellow of plain and uncoined constancy; for he perforce must do thee right, because he hath not the gift to woo in other places: for these fellows of infinite tongue, that can rhyme themselves into ladies' favours, they do always reason themselves out again. What! a speaker is but a prater; a rhyme is but a ballad. A good leg will fall; a straight back will stoop; a black beard will turn white; a curled pate will grow bald; a fair face will wither; a full eye will wax hollow: but a good heart, Kate, is the sun and the moon; or rather the sun and not the moon; for it shines bright and never changes, but keeps his course truly. If thou would have such a one, take me; and take me, take a soldier; take a soldier, take a king.
King Henry—Henry V V.ii

What power is it which mounts my love so high,
That makes me see, and cannot feed mine eye?

The mightiest space in fortune nature brings
To join like likes and kiss like native things.

Helena—All's Well I.i

My friends were poor but honest, so's my love.

Helena—All's Well I.iii

This love will undo us all. O
Cupid, Cupid, Cupid!

Helen—TC III.i

I love her;
But, saying thus, instead of oil and balm,
Thou lay'st in every gash that love hath given me
The knife that made it.

Troilus—TC I.i

I stalk about her door,
Like a strange soul upon the Stygian banks
Staying for waftage.

Troilus—TC III.ii

I am giddy; expectation whirls me round,
Th' imaginary relish is so sweet
That it enchants my sense: what will it be,
When that the wat'ry palates taste indeed
Love's thrice reputed nectar?

Troilus—TC III.ii

My heart beats thicker than a feverous pulse;
And all my powers do their bestowing lose,
Like vassalage at unawares encount'ring
The eye of majesty.

Troilus—TC III.ii

That is the monstruosity in love, lady, that the will is infinite and the execution confined, that the desire is boundless and the act a slave to limit.   *Troilus—TC III.ii*

They say all lovers swear more performance than they are able and yet reserve an ability that they never perform, vowing more than the perfection of ten and discharging less than the tenth part of one.   *Cressida—TC III.ii*

> I love thee in so strain'd a purity,
> That the bless'd gods, as angry with my fancy,
> More bright in zeal than the devotion which
> Cold lips blow to their deities, take thee from me.
> *Troilus—TC IV.iv*

> Perdition catch my soul,
> But I do love thee! and when I love thee not,
> Chaos is come again.   *Othello—Othello III.iii*

> When you sued staying,
> Then was the time for words: no going then;
> Eternity was in our lips and eyes,
> Bliss in our brows' bent; none our parts so poor,
> But was a race of heaven.   *Cleopatra—A&C I.iii*

> O thou day o' th' world,
> Chain mine arm'd neck; leap thou, attire and all,
> Through proof of harness to my heart, and there
> Ride on the pants triumphing!   *Antony—A&C IV.viii*

> I am dying, Egypt, dying; only
> I here importune death awhile, until
> Of many thousand kisses the poor last
> I lay upon thy lips.   *Antony—A&C IV.xv*

For my sake wear this;
It is a manacle of love; I'll place it
Upon the fairest prisoner.   *Posthumus—Cymbeline I.i*

M

MANHOOD: "Do you know a man if you see him?"

A man is master of his liberty,
Time is their master, and when they see time
They'll go or come.   *Luciana—CE II.i*

There's nothing situate under heaven's eye
But hath his bound, in earth, in sea, in sky:
The beasts, the fishes, and the winged fowls
Are their males' subjects and at their controls:
Man, more divine, the master of all these,
Lord of the wide world and wild watery seas,
Indued with intellectual sense and souls,
Of more preeminence than fish and fowls,
Are masters to their females, and their lords.
                                        Luciana—CE II.i

He cannot be a perfect man,
Not being tried and tutor'd in the world:
Experience is by industry achieved
And perfected by the swift course of time.
                                        Antonio—TGV I.iii

O heaven! Were man
But constant, he were perfect. That one error
Fills him with faults; makes him run through all th' sins:
Inconstancy falls off ere it begins.   *Proteus—TGV V.iv*

What is the trust or strength of foolish man?
They that of late were daring with their scoffs
Are glad and fain by flight to save themselves.
Bedford—1 Henry VI III.ii

Small things make base men proud.
Suffolk—2 Henry VI IV.i

For many men that stumble at the threshold
Are well foretold that danger waits within.
Gloucester—3 Henry VI IV.vii

Great lords, wise men ne'er sit and wail their loss,
But cheerly seek how to redress their harms.
Queen—3 Henry VI V.iv

Talkers are no good doers.
First Murderer—Richard III I.iii

Princes have but their titles for their glories,
An outward honour for an inward toil;
And, for unfelt imaginations,
They often feel a world of restless cares;
So that, between their titles and low name,
There's nothing differs but the outward fame.
Brakenbury—Richard III I.iv

By a divine instinct men's minds mistrust
Ensuing danger; as, by a proof, we see
The water swell before a boist'rous storm.
Third Citizen—Richard III II.iii

O momentary grace of mortal men,
Which we more hunt for than the grace of God!

Who builds his hope in air of your good looks,
Lives like a drunken sailor on a mast,
Ready, with every nod, to tumble down
Into the fatal bowels of the deep.

Hastings—Richard III III.iv

Men shall deal unadvisedly sometimes,
Which after hours gives leisure to repent.

Richard—Richard III IV.iv

Lady, such a man
As all the world—why he's a man of wax.   *Nurse—RJ I.iii*

Art thou a man? thy form cries out thou art;
Thy tears are womanish; thy wild acts denote
The unreasonable fury of a beast:
Unseemly woman in a seeming man!
And ill-seeming beast in seeming both!

Friar Laurence—RJ III.iii

O mischief, thou art swift,
To enter in the thoughts of desperate men!   *Romeo—RJ V.i*

Nature hath fram'd strange fellows in her time:
Some that will evermore peep through their eyes
And laugh like parrots at a bag-piper,
And other of such vinegar aspect
That they'll not show their teeth in way of smile,
Though Nestor swear the jest be laughable.

Solanio—MV I.i

There are a sort of men whose visages
Do cream and mantle like a standing pond,
And do a willful stillness entertain,

With purpose to be dress'd in an opinion
Of wisdom, gravity, profound conceit,
As who should say 'I am Sir Oracle,
And when I ope my lips let no dog bark!'

Gratiano—MV I.i

He wears his faith but as the fashion of his hat; it ever changes with the next block.   *Beatrice—Much Ado I.i*

That a woman conceived me, I thank her: that she brought me up, I likewise give her most humble thanks: but that I will have a recheat winded in my forehead, or hang my bugle in an invisible baldrick, all women shall pardon me.

Benedick—Much Ado I.i

But doth not the appetite alter? A man loves the meat in his youth that he cannot endure in his age. Shall quips and sentences and these paper bullets of the brain awe a man from the career of his humour? No, the world must be peopled.

Benedick—Much Ado II.iii

O, what men dare do! What men may do! What men daily do, not knowing what they do!   *Claudio—Much Ado IV.i*

Manhood is melted into courtesies, valour into compliment, and men are only turned into tongue, and trim ones too: he is now as valiant as Hercules that only tells a lie and swears it.   *Beatrice—Much Ado IV.i*

'Tis all men's office to speak patience
To those that wring under the load of sorrow,
But no man's virtue nor sufficiency
To be so moral when he shall endure
The like himself.   *Leonato—Much Ado V.i*

I will find you twenty lascivious turtles ere one chaste man.
Mrs. Page—Merry Wives II.i

A kind heart he hath: a woman would run through fire and water for such a kind heart.   *Quickly—Merry Wives III.iv*

What shall he have that kill'd the deer?
His leather skin and horns to wear.
       Then sing him home;
Take thou no scorn to wear the horn;
It was a crest ere thou wast born:
       Thy father's father wore it,
       And thy father bore it:
The horn, the horn, the lusty horn
Is not a thing to laugh to scorn.   *Foresters—AYLI IV.ii*

I hate ingratitude more in a man
Than lying, vainness, babbling, drunkenness,
Or any taint of vice whose strong corruption
Inhabits our frail blood.   *Viola—TN III.iv*

To be said an honest man and a good housekeeper goes as fairly as to say a careful man and a great scholar.
Feste—TN IV.ii

When thou art king, let not us that are squires of the night's body be called thieves of the day's beauty: let us be Diana's foresters, gentlemen of the shade, minions of the moon: and let men say we be men of good government, being governed, as the sea is, by our noble and chaste mistress the moon, under whose countenance we steal.
Falstaff—1 Henry IV I.ii

There lives not three good men unhanged in England: and one of them is fat and grows old. *Falstaff—1 Henry IV II.iv*

If sack and sugar be a fault, God help the wicked! if to be old and merry be a sin, then many an old host that I know is damned; if to be fat be to be hated, then Pharaoh's lean kine are to be loved. *Falstaff—1 Henry IV II.iv*

O, he is as tedious
As a tired horse, a railing wife;
Worse than a smoky house; I had rather live
With cheese and garlic in a windmill, far,
Than feed on cates and have him talk to me
In any summer-house in Christendom.
Hotspur—I Henry IV III.i

Tut, never fear me: I am as vigilant as a cat to steal cream.
Falstaff—1 Henry IV IV.ii

O thoughts of men accurs'd!
Past and to come seems best; things present worst.
Archbishop—2 Henry IV I.iii

He was indeed the glass
Wherein the noble youth did dress themselves.
Lady Percy—2 Henry IV II.iii

There's never none of these demure boys come to any proof; for thin drink doth so over-cool their blood, and making many fish-meals, that they fall into a kind of male green-sickness; and then when they marry, they get wenches: they are generally fools and cowards; which some of us should be too, but for inflammation. A good sherris-sack hath a two-fold operation in it. It ascends me into the brain; dries me there all the foolish and dull and crudy vapours which environ it; makes it apprehensive, quick, forgetive, full of nimble fiery and delectable shapes; which, delivered o'er to the voice, the tongue, which is the birth, becomes excellent wit. The second property of your excellent sherris is, the warming of the blood; which, before cold and settled, left the liver white and pale, which is the badge of pusillanimity and cowardice; but the sherris warms it and makes it course from the inwards to the parts extreme: it illumineth the face, which as a beacon gives warning to all the rest of this little kingdom, man, to arm; and then the vital commoners and inland petty spirits muster me all to their captain, the heart, who, great and puffed up with this retinue, doth any deed of courage; and this valour comes of sherris. So that skill in the weapon is nothing without sack, for that sets it a-work; and learning a mere hoard of gold kept by a devil, till sack commences it and sets it in act and use.   *Falstaff—2 Henry IV IV.iii*

Self-love, my liege, is not so vile a sin
As self-neglecting.   *Dauphin—Henry V II.iv*

I think the king is but a man, as I am: the violet smells to him as it doth to me; the element shows to him as it doth to me; all his senses have but human conditions: his ceremonies laid by, in his nakedness he appears but a man; and though his affections are higher mounted than ours, yet, when they stoop, they stoop with the like wing.
                                      King Henry—Henry V IV.i

I did never know so full a voice issue from so empty a heart; but the saying is true, 'The empty vessel makes the greatest sound.'   *Boy—Henry V IV.iv*

This was the noblest Roman of them all:
All the conspirators save only he
Did that they did in envy of great Caesar;
He only, in a general honest thought
And common good to all, made one of them.
His life was gentle, and the elements
So mix'd in him that Nature might stand up
And say to all the world 'This was a man!'   *Antony—JC V.v*

There can be no kernel in this light nut; the soul of this man
is his clothes.   *Lafeu—All's Well II.v*

A man whose blood
Is very snow-broth; one who never feels
The wanton stings and motions of the sense,
But doth rebate and blunt his natural edge
With profits of the mind, study and fast.   *Lucio—MforM I.iv*

O place, O form,
How often dost thou with thy case, thy habit,
Wrench awe from fools and tie the wiser souls
To thy false seeming! Blood, thou art blood:
Let's write good angel on the devil's horn;
'Tis not the devil's crest.   *Angelo—MforM II.iv*

Every true man's apparel fits your thief: if it be too little for
your thief, your true man thinks it big enough; if it be too
big for your thief, your thief thinks it little enough: so every
true man's apparel fits your thief.   *Abhorson—MforM IV.ii*

Do you know a man if you see him?
Pandarus—TC I.ii

Do you know what a man is? Is not birth, beauty, good shape, discourse, manhood, learning, gentleness, virtue, youth, liberality, and such like, the spice and salt that season a man?

Pandarus—TC I.ii

'Tis certain, greatness, once fall'n out with fortune,
Must fall out with men too: what the declin'd is
He shall as soon read in the eyes of others
As feel in his own fall.   *Achilles—TC III.iii*

                    O heavens, what some men do,
While some men leave to do!
How some men creep in skittish fortune's hall,
Whiles others play the idiots in her eyes!
How one man eats into another's pride,
While pride is fasting in his wantonness!

Ulysses—TC III.iii

So, oft it chances in particular men,
That for some vicious mole of nature in them,
As, in their birth—wherein they are not guilty,
Since nature cannot choose his origin—
By the o'ergrowth of some complexion,
Oft breaking down the pales and forts of reason,
Or by some habit that too much o'er-leavens
The form of plausive manners, that these men,
Carrying, I say, the stamp of one defect,
Being nature's livery, or fortune's star,—
Their virtues else—be they as pure as grace,
As infinite as man may undergo—
Shall in the general censure take corruption
From that particular fault.   *Hamlet—Hamlet I.iv*

Though this be madness, yet there is method in 't.
Polonius—Hamlet II.ii

O, what a noble mind is here o'erthrown!
The courtier's, soldier's, scholar's, eye, tongue, sword!
Th' expectancy and rose of the fair state,
The glass of fashion and the mould of form,
Th' observ'd of all observers, quite, quite down!
Ophelia—Hamlet III.ii

How all occasions do inform against me,
And spur my dull revenge! What is a man,
If his chief good and market of his time
Be but to sleep and feed? a beast no more.
Sure, he that made us with such large discourse
Looking before and after, gave us not
That capability and god-like reason
To fust in us unus'd. Now, whether it be
Bestial oblivion, or some craven scruple
Of thinking too precisely on th' event,
A thought which, quarter'd, hath but one part wisdom
And ever three parts coward, I do not know
Why yet I live to say 'This thing's to do,'
Since I have cause and will and strength and means
To do 't.
Hamlet—Hamlet IV.iv

He is the brooch indeed
And gem of all the nation.
Laertes—Hamlet IV.vii

Men should be what they seem:
Or those that be not, would they might seem none!
Iago—Othello III.iii

Go to, they are not men o' their words: they told me I was
everything; 'tis a lie, I am not ague-proof.   *Lear—Lear IV.vi*

I cannot draw a cart, nor eat dried oats;
If it be man's work, I'll do't.   *Captain—Lear V.iii*

Who dares, who dares,

In purity of manhood stand upright,
And say, 'This man's a flatterer'? if one be,
So are they all; for every grise of fortune
Is smooth'd by that below: the learned pate
Ducks to the golden fool: all's obliquy;
There's nothing level in our cursed natures,
But direct villany. Therefore, be abhorr'd
All feasts, societies, and throngs of men!
Timon—Timon IV.iii

Present fears

Are less than horrible imaginings:
My thought, whose murder yet is but fantastical,
Shakes so my single state of man that function
Is smother'd in surmise, and nothing is
But what is not.   *Macbeth—Macbeth I.iii*

I dare do all that may become a man;
Who dares do more is none.   *Macbeth—Macbeth I.vii*

Where we are,

There's daggers in men's smiles: the near in blood,
The nearer bloody.   *Donalbain—Macbeth II.iii*

Thriftless ambition, that will ravin up
Thine own life's means!   *Ross—Macbeth II.iv*

You shall find there
A man who is the abstract of all faults
That all men follow.   *Caesar—A&C I.iv*

A rarer spirit never
Did steer humanity; but you, gods, will give us
Some faults to make us men.   *Agrippa—A&C V.i*

What would you have, you curs,
That like nor peace nor war? the one affrights you,
The other makes you proud. He that trusts to you,
Where he should find you lions, finds you hares;
Where foxes, geese: you are no surer, no,
Than is the coal of fire upon the ice,
Or hailstone in the sun.   *Marcius—Coriolanus I.i*

But now 'tis odds beyond arithmetic;
And manhood is call'd foolery, when it stands
Against a falling fabric.   *Cominius—Coriolanus III.i*

He is their god: he leads them like a thing
Made by some other deity than nature,
That shapes man better; and they follow him,
Against us brats, with no less confidence
Than boys pursuing summer butterflies,
Or butchers killing flies.   *Cominius—Coriolanus IV.vi*

They do abuse the king that flatter him:
For flattery is the bellows blows up sin;
The thing the which is flattered, but a spark,
To which that blast gives heat and stronger glowing;
Whereas reproof, obedient and in order,
Fits kings, as they are men, for they may err.
                    Helicanus—Pericles I.ii

> For princes are
> A model, which heaven makes like to itself:
> As jewels lose their glory if neglected,
> So princes their renowns if not respected.
>
> *Simonides—Pericles II.ii*

> This is the state of man: today he puts forth
> The tender leaves of hopes; to-morrow blossoms,
> And bears his blushing honours thick upon him;
> The third day comes a frost, a killing frost,
> And, when he thinks, good easy man, full surely
> His greatness is a-ripening, nips his root,
> And then he falls.   *Wolsey—Henry VIII III.ii*

> Men that make
> Envy and crooked malice nourishment
> Dare bite the best.   *Cranmer—Henry VIII V.iii*

> Men so noble,
> However faulty, yet should find respect
> For what they have been: 'tis a cruelty
> To load a falling man.   *Cromwell—Henry VIII V.iii*

> Men are mad things.
>
> *Emilia—TNK II.ii*

MARRIAGE: "Get thee a wife, get thee a wife"

> Thou art an elm, my husband, I a vine,
> Whose weakness married to thy stronger state
> Makes me with thy strength to communicate:
>
> *Adriana—CE II.ii*

My wife is shrewish when I keep not hours.
Antipholus of Ephesus—CE III.i

I knew a wench married in an afternoon as she went to the
garden for parsley to stuff a rabbit.   *Biondello—TS IV.iv*

When daisies pied and violets blue
     And lady-smocks all silver-white
And cuckoo-buds of yellow hue
     Do paint the meadows with delight,
The cuckoo then, on every tree,
Mocks married men; for thus sings he, Cuckoo;
Cuckoo, cuckoo: O word of fear,
Unpleasing to a married ear!   *Armado—LLL V.ii*

Marriage is a matter of more worth
Than to be dealt in by attorneyship.
Suffolk—1 Henry VI V.v

For what is wedlock forced but a hell,
An age of discord and continual strife?
Whereas the contrary bringeth bliss,
And is a pattern of celestial peace.   *Suffolk—1 Henry VI V.v*

     Yet hasty marriage seldom proveth well.
Gloucester—3 Henry VI IV.i

He is the half part of a blessed man,
Left to be finished by such as she;
And she a fair divided excellence,
Whose fullness of perfection lies in him.
O, two such silver currents, when they join,
Do glorify the banks that bound them in.
First Citizen—King John II.i

She's not well married that lives married long;
But she's best married that dies married young.

Friar Laurence—RJ IV.v

Let me not to the marriage of true minds
Admit impediments. Love is not love
Which alters when it alteration finds,
Or bends with the remover to remove.
O, no! it is an ever fixed mark
That looks on tempests and is never shaken;
It is the star to every wand'ring bark,
Whose worth's unknown, although his height be taken.
Love's not Time's fool, though rosy lips and cheeks
Within his bending sickle's compass come;
Love alters not with his brief hours and weeks,
But bears it out even to the edge of doom:
    If this be error and upon me prov'd,
    I never writ, nor no man ever lov'd.   *Sonnet 116*

The ancient saying is no heresy,
Hanging and wiving goes by destiny.   *Nerissa—MV II.ix*

Shall I never see a bachelor of threescore again? Go to, i'
faith; an thou wilt needs thrust thy neck into a yoke, wear
the print of it and sigh away Sundays.

Benedick—Much Ado I.i

Lord, I could not endure a husband with a beard on his
face: I had rather lie in the woollen.

Beatrice—Much Ado II.i

He that hath a beard is more than a youth, and he that hath
no beard is less than a man: and he that is more than a
youth is not for me, and he that is less than a man, I am not
for him.   *Beatrice—Much Ado II.i*

Wooing, wedding, and repenting, is as a Scotch jig, a measure, and a cinque pace: the first suit is hot and hasty, like a Scotch jig, and full as fantastical; the wedding, mannerly-modest, as a measure, full of state and ancientry; and then comes Repentance and, with his bad legs, falls into the cinque pace faster and faster, till he sink into the grave.

Beatrice—Much Ado II.i

Is not marriage honourable in a beggar?

Margaret—Much Ado III.iv

Since I do purpose to marry, I will think nothing to any purpose that the world can say against it; and therefore never flout at me for what I have said against it; for man is a giddy thing. *Benedick—Much Ado V.iv*

Get thee a wife, get thee a wife; there is no staff more reverend than one tipped with horn. *Benedick—Much Ado V.iv*

If there be no great love in the beginning, yet heaven may decrease it upon better acquaintance, when we are married and have more occasion to know one another; I hope, upon familiarity will grow more contempt.

Slender—Merry Wives I.i

In love the heavens themselves do guide the state;
Money buys lands, and wives are sold by fate.

Ford—Merry Wives V.v

Is the single man therefore blessed? No: as a walled town is more worthier than a village, so is the forehead of a married man more honourable than the bare brow of a bachelor; and by how much defence is better than no skill, by so much is a horn more precious than to want. *Touchstone—AYLI III.iii*

Men are April when they woo, December when they wed:
maids are May when they are maids, but the sky changes
when they are wives.   *Rosalind—AYLI IV.i*

I press in here, sir, amongst the rest of the country copula-
tives, to swear and to forswear; according as marriage
binds and blood breaks: a poor virgin, sir, an ill-favoured
thing, sir, but mine own; a poor humour of mine, sir, to take
that that no man else will; rich honesty dwells like a miser,
sir, in a poor house; as your pearl in your foul oyster.
                                                Touchstone—AYLI V.iv

Wedding is great Juno's crown,
    O blessed bond of board and bed:
'Tis Hymen peoples every town;
    High wedlock then be honoured:
Honour, high honour and renown,
    To Hymen, god of every town!   *Hymen—AYLI V.iv*

       Let still the woman take
An elder than herself; so wears she to him
So sways she level in her husband's heart:
For, boy, however we do praise ourselves,
Our fancies are more giddy and unfirm,
More longing, wavering, sooner lost and worn,
Than women's are.   *Orsino—TN II.iv*

Within the bond of marriage, tell me Brutus,
Is it excepted I should know no secrets
That appertain to you? Am I yourself
But, as it were, in sort or limitation,
To keep with you at meals, comfort your bed,
And talk to you sometimes? Dwell I but in the suburbs
Of your good pleasure?   *Portia—JC II.i*

He that comforts my wife is the cherisher of my flesh and blood; he that cherishes my flesh and blood loves my flesh and blood; he that loves my flesh and blood is my friend: ergo, he that kisses my wife is my friend. If men could be contented to be what they are, there were no fear in marriage.

Clown—All's Well I.iii

For I the ballad will repeat,
  Which men full true shall find;
Your marriage comes by destiny,
  Your cuckoo sings by kind.   *Clown—All's Well I.iii*

A young man married is a man that's marred.

Parolles—All's Well II.iii

They say, best men are moulded out of faults;
And, for the most, become much more the better
For being a little bad: so may my husband.

Mariana—MforM V.i

Nature craves
All dues be rend'red to their owners: now,
What nearer debt in all humanity
Than wife is to the husband?   *Hector—TC II.ii*

Happiness to their sheets!   *Iago—Othello II.iii*

O curse of marriage,
That we can call these delicate creatures ours,
And not their appetites.   *Othello—Othello III.iii*

'Tis not a year or two shows us a man:
They are all but stomachs, and we all but food;
They eat us hungerly, and when they are full,
They belch us.   *Emilia—Othello III.iv*

Who would not make her husband a cuckold to make him a monarch? I should venture purgatory for 't.

Emilia—Othello IV.iii

But I do think it is their husbands' faults
If wives do fall: say that they slack their duties,
And pour our treasures into foreign laps,
Or else break out in peevish jealousies,
Throwing restraint upon us; or say they strike us,
Or scant our former having in despite;
Why, we have galls, and though we have some grace,
Yet have we some revenge. Let husbands know
Their wives have sense like them: they see and smell
And have their palates both for sweet and sour,
As husbands have. What is it that they do
When they change us for others? Is it sport?
I think it is: and doth affection breed it?
I think it doth: is't frailty that thus errs?
It is so too: and have not we affections,
Desires for sport, and frailty, as man have?
Then let them use us well: else let them know,
The ills we do, their ills instruct us so.

Emilia—Othello IV.iii

As it is a heart-breaking to see a handsome man loose-wived, so it is a deadly sorrow to behold a foul knave un-cuckolded.

Iras—A&C I.ii

The fittest time to corrupt a man's wife is when she's fallen out with her husband.

Roman—Coriolanus IV.iii

For your bride goes to that with shame which is her way to go with warrant.

Bawd—Pericles IV.ii

There have been,
Or I am much deceiv'd, cuckolds ere now;
And many a man there is, even at this present,
Now while I speak this, holds his wife by th' arm,
And little thinks she has been sluic'd in 's absence
And his pond fish'd by his next neighbour,
By Sir Smile, his neighbour.   *Leontes—WT I.ii*

Should all despair
That have revolted wives, the tenth of mankind
Would hang themselves. Physic for 't there's none;
It is a bawdy planet.   *Leontes—WT I.ii*

Honour, riches, marriage-blessing,
Long continuance, and increasing,
Hourly joys be still upon you!
Juno sings her blessings on you.
            Juno and Ceres—Tempest IV.i

I am bride-habited,
But maiden-hearted.   *Emilia—TNK V.i*

MORTALITY: "Death is a fearful thing"

Grim death, how foul and loathsome is thy image!
            Lord—TS Induction.i

But now the arbitrator of despairs,
Just death, kind umpire of men's miseries,
With sweet enlargement doth dismiss me hence.
            Mortimer—1 Henry VI II.v

But kings and mightiest potentates must die,
For that's the end of human misery.

Talbot—1 Henry VI III.ii

My joy is death;
Death, at whose name I oft have been afear'd,
Because I wish'd this world's eternity.

Duchess—2 Henry VI II.iv

To die by thee were but to die in jest;
From thee to die were torture more than death.

Suffolk—2 Henry VI III.ii

Ah, what a sign it is of evil life,
Where death's approach is seen so terrible!

King—2 Henry VI III.iii

O Lord! methought, what pain it was to drown!
What dreadful noise of water in mine ears!
What sights of ugly death within mine eyes!
Methoughts I saw a thousand fearful wracks;
A thousand men that fishes gnaw'd upon.

Clarence—Richard III I.iv

It were lost sorrow to wail one that's lost.

Duchess of York—Richard III II.ii

Why grow the branches when the root is gone?
Why wither not the leaves that want their sap?

Queen Elizabeth—Richard III II.ii

'Tis a vile thing to die, my gracious lord,
When men are unprepar'd and look not for it.

Catesby—Richard III III.ii

So now prosperity begins to mellow
And drop into the rotten mouth of death.
Queen Margaret—Richard III IV.iv

Death, death; O amiable lovely death!
Thou odoriferous stench! sound rottenness!
Arise forth from the couch of lasting night,
Thou hate and terror to prosperity,
And I will kiss thy detestable bones
And put my eyeballs in thy vaulty brows
And ring these fingers with thy household worms
And stop this gap of breath with fulsome dust
And be a carrion monster like thyself:
Come, grin on me, and I will think thou smil'st
And buss thee as thy wife. Misery's love,
O, come to me! *Constance—King John III.iv*

Death, having prey'd upon the outward parts,
Leaves them invisible, and his siege is now
Against the mind, the which he pricks and wounds
With many legions of strange fantasies,
Which, in their throng and press to that last hold,
Confound themselves. 'Tis strange that death should sing.
Prince Henry—King John V.vii

Ay, marry, now my soul hath elbow-room;
It would not out at windows nor at doors.
There is so hot a summer in my bosom,
That all my bowels crumble up to dust:
King John—King John V.vii

Ask for me tomorrow, and you shall find me a grave man. I
am peppered, I warrant, for this world. A plague o' both
your houses! 'Zounds, a dog, a rat, a mouse, a cat, to scratch

a man to death! a braggart, a rogue, a villain, that fights by
the book of arithmetic!   *Mercutio—RJ III.i*

Death lies on her like an untimely frost
Upon the sweetest flower of all the field.   *Capulet—RJ IV.v*

How oft when men are at the point of death
Have they been merry! which their keepers call
A lightning before death.   *Romeo—RJ V.iii*

Eyes, look your last!
Arms, take your last embrace! and, lips, O you
The doors of breath, seal with a righteous kiss
A dateless bargain to engrossing death!   *Romeo—RJ V.iii*

I am a tainted wether of the flock,
Meetest for death: the weakest kind of fruit
Drops earliest to the ground; and so let me.
                                       Antonio—MV IV.i

If a man do not erect in this age his own tomb ere he dies, he
shall live no longer in monument than the bell rings and the
widow weeps.   *Benedick—Much Ado V.ii*

Come away, come away, death,
    And in sad cypress let me be laid;
Fly away, fly away, breath;
    I am slain by a fair cruel maid.
My shroud of white, stuck all with yew,
    O, prepare it!
My part of death, no one so true
    Did share it.

Not a flower, not a flower sweet,
    On my black coffin let there by strown;

Not a friend, not a friend greet
　　My poor corpse, where my bones shall be thrown;
A thousand thousand sighs to save,
　　Lay me, O, where
Sad true lover never find my grave,
　　　　To weep there!　　　　　　　*Feste—TN II.iv*

O, but they say the tongues of dying men
Enforce attention like deep harmony:
Where words are scarce, they are seldom spent in vain,
For they breathe truth that breathe their words in pain.
He that no more must say is listened more
Than they whom youth and ease have taught to glose;
More are men's ends mark'd than their lives before:
The setting sun, and music at the close,
As the last taste of sweets, is sweetest last,
Writ in remembrance more than things long past.
　　　　　　　John of Gaunt—Richard II II.i

The ripest fruit first falls, and so doth he;
His time is spent.　　　　　*King Richard—Richard II II.i*

Cry woe, destruction, ruin and decay:
The worst is death and death will have his day.
　　　　　　　King Richard—Richard II III.ii

For God's sake, let us sit upon the ground
And tell sad stories of the death of kings:
How some have been depos'd; some slain in war;
Some haunted by the ghosts they have depos'd;
Some poisoned by their wives; some sleeping kill'd;
All murdered: for within the hollow crown
That rounds the mortal temples of a king
Keeps Death his court and there the antic sits,
Scoffing his state and grinning at his pomp,

Allowing him a breath, a little scene,
To monarchize, be fear'd and kill with looks,
Infusing him with self and vain conceit,
As if this flesh which walls about our life
Were brass impregnable, and humour'd thus
Comes at the last and with a little pin
Bores through his castle wall, and farewell king!
King Richard—Richard II III.ii

Mount, mount, my soul! thy seat is up on high;
Whilst my gross flesh sinks downward, here to die.
King Richard—Richard II V.v

Doomsday is near; die all, die merrily.
Hotspur—1 Henry IV IV.i

But thought's the slave of life, and life time's fool;
And time, that takes survey of all the world,
Must have a stop.   *Hotspur—1 Henry IV V.iv*

Fare thee well, great heart!
Ill-weav'd ambition, how much art thou shrunk!
When that this body did contain a spirit,
A kingdom for it was too small a bound;
But now two paces of the vilest earth
Is room enough: this earth that bears thee dead
Bears not alive so stout a gentleman.
Prince—1 Henry IV V.iv

To die, is to be a counterfeit; for he is but the counterfeit of a
man who hath not the life of a man: but to counterfeit
dying, when a man thereby liveth, is to be no counterfeit,
but the true and perfect image of life indeed. The better part

of valour is discretion; in the which better part I have saved
my life.   *Falstaff—1 Henry IV V.iv*

Then death rock me asleep, abridge my doleful days!
                                            Pistol—2 Henry IV II.iv

A man can die but once; we owe God a death: I'll ne'er bear
a base mind: an't be my destiny, so; an't be not, so: no man's
too good to serve's prince; and let it go which way it will, he
that dies this year is quit for the next.
                                            Feeble—2 Henry IV III.ii

I am afeard there are few die well that die in a battle; for
how can they charitably dispose of any thing, when blood
is their argument? Now, if these men do not die well, it will
be a black matter for the king that led them to it.
                                            Will—Henry V IV.i

The king is not bound to answer the particular endings of
his soldiers, the father of his son, nor the master of his servant; for they purpose not their death, when they purpose
their services.   *King Henry—Henry V IV.i*

Every subject's duty is the king's; but every subject's soul is
his own. Therefore should every soldier in the wars do as
every sick man in his bed, wash every mote out of his conscience: and dying so, death is to him advantage; or not
dying, the time was blessedly lost wherein such preparation was gained.   *King Henry—Henry V IV.i*

When beggars die, there are no comets seen;
The heavens themselves blaze forth the death of princes.
                                            Calpurnia—JC II.ii

Cowards die many times before their deaths;
The valiant never taste of death but once.
Of all the wonders that I yet have heard,
It seems to me most strange that men should fear;
Seeing that death, a necessary end,
Will come when it will come.   *Caesar—JC II.ii*

Why, he that cuts off twenty years of life
Cuts off so many years of fearing death.   *Cassius—JC III.i*

                  'Let me not live,' quoth he,
'After my flame lacks oil, to be the snuff
Of younger spirits, whose apprehensive senses
All but new things disdain; whose judgements are
Mere fathers of their garments; whose constancies
Expire before their fashions.'   *King—All's Well I.ii*

                  Dar'st thou die?
The sense of death is most in apprehension;
And the poor beetle, that we tread upon,
In corporal sufferance finds a pang as great
As when a giant dies.   *Isabella—MforM III.i*

                  Death is a fearful thing.
                        Claudio—MforM III.i

Ay, but to die, and go we know not where;
To lie in cold obstruction and to rot;
This sensible warm motion to become
A kneaded clod; and the delighted spirit
To bathe in fiery floods, or to reside
In thrilling region of thick-ribbed ice;
To be imprison'd in the viewless winds,
And blown with restless violence round about

The pendent world; or to be worse than worst
Of those that lawless and incertain thought
Imagine howling: 'tis too horrible!
The weariest and most loathed worldly life
That age, ache, penury and imprisonment
Can lay on nature is a paradise
To what we fear of death.   *Claudio—MforM III.i*

Your worm is your only emperor for diet: we fat all creatures else to fat us, and we fat ourselves for maggots: your
fat king and your lean beggar is but variable service, two
dishes, but to one table: that's the end.
          Hamlet—Hamlet IV.iii

Why may not that be the skull of a lawyer? Where be his
quiddities now, his quillities, his cases, his tenures, and his
tricks? why does he suffer this mad knave now to knock
him about the sconce with a dirty shovel, and will not tell
him of his action of battery? Hum! This fellow might be in 's
time a great buyer of land, with his statutes, his recog-
nizances, his fines, his double vouchers, his recoveries: is
this the fine of his fines, and the recovery of his recoveries,
to have his fine pate full of fine dirt? will his vouchers
vouch him no more of his purchases, and double ones too,
than the length and breadth of a pair of indentures? The
very conveyance of his lands will scarcely lie in this box;
and must the inheritor himself have no more, ha?
          Hamlet—Hamlet V.i

Alas, poor Yorick! I knew him, Horatio: a fellow of infinite
jest, of most excellent fancy: he hath borne me on his back a
thousand times; and now, how abhorred in my imagination
it is! my gorge rises at it. Here hung those lips that I have
kissed I know not how oft. Where be your gibes now? your

gambols? your songs? your flashes of merriment, that were
wont to set the table on a roar? Not one now, to mock your
own grinning? quite chap-fallen? Now get you to my lady's
chamber, and tell her, let her paint an inch thick, to this
favour she must come; make her laugh at that.

Hamlet—Hamlet V.i

Imperious Caesar, dead and turn'd to clay,
Might stop a hole to keep the wind away:
O, that that earth, which kept the world in awe,
Should patch a wall t'expel the winter's flaw!

Hamlet—Hamlet V.i

Sweets to the sweet: farewell!

Gertrude—Hamlet V.i

Had I but time—as this fell sergeant, Death,
Is strict in his arrest—O, I could tell you—
But let it be.   *Hamlet—Hamlet V.ii*

The rest is silence.

Hamlet—Hamlet V.ii

Now cracks a noble heart. Good night, sweet prince;
And flights of angels sing thee to thy rest!

Horatio—Hamlet V.ii

Men must endure
Their going hence, even as their coming hither:
Ripeness is all.   *Edgar—Lear V.ii*

O, our lives' sweetness!
That we the pain of death would hourly die
Rather than die at once!   *Edgar—Lear V.iii*

Why should a dog, a horse, a rat, have life,
And thou no breath at all? Thou'lt come no more,
Never, never, never, never, never!   *Lear—Lear V.iii*

Nothing in his life
Became him like the leaving it; he died
As one that had been studied in his death
To throw away the dearest thing he ow'd,
As 'twere a careless trifle.   *Malcolm—Macbeth I.iv*

Noblest of men, woo't die?
Hast thou no care of me? shall I abide
In this dull world, which in thy absence is
No better than a sty? O, see, my women,
The crown o' the earth doth melt. My lord!
O, wither'd is the garland of the war,
The soldier's pole is fall'n: young boys and girls
Are level now with men; the odds is gone,
And there is nothing left remarkable
Beneath the visiting moon.   *Cleopatra—A&C IV.xv*

For death remembered should be like a mirror,
Who tells us life's but breath, to trust it error.
          Pericles—Pericles I.i

Fear no more the heat o' the sun,
     Nor the furious winter's rages;
Thou thy worldly task hast done,
     Home art gone, and ta'en thy wages:
Golden lads and girls all must,
As chimney sweepers, come to dust.

Fear no more the frown of the great;
     Thou art past the tyrant's stroke;

Care no more to clothe or eat;
    To thee the reed is as the oak.
The sceptre, learning, physic, must
All follow this, and come to dust.

Fear no more the lightning flash,
    Nor the all-dreaded thunder-stone;
Fear not slander, censure rash;
    Thou hast finish'd joy and moan:
All lovers young, all lovers must
Consign to thee, and come to dust.

No exorciser harm thee!
    Nor no witchcraft charm thee!
Ghost unlaid forbear thee!
    Nothing ill come near thee!
Quiet consummation have;
And renowned be thy grave!
                    Guiderius, Arviragus—Cymbeline IV.ii

The herbs that have on them cold dew o' th' night
Are strewings fitt'st for graves.
                    Belarius—Cymbeline IV.ii

The comfort is, you shall be called to no more payments,
fear no more tavern-bills; which are often the sadness of
parting, as the procuring of mirth: you come in faint for
want of meat, depart reeling with too much drink; sorry
that you have paid too much, and sorry that you are paid
too much; purse and brain both empty; the brain the heav-
ier for being too light, the purse too light, being drawn of
heaviness: of this contradiction you shall now be quit. O,
the charity of a penny cord! it sums up thousands in a trice:
you have no true debitor and creditor but it; of what's past,

is, and to come, the discharge: your neck, sir, is pen, book
and counters; so the acquittance follows.

First Gaoler—Cymbeline V.iv

By med'cine life may be prolong'd, yet death
Will seize the doctor too.   *Cymbeline—Cymbeline V.v*

He that dies pays all debts.   *Stephano—Tempest III.ii*

O my good lord, that comfort comes too late;
'Tis like a pardon after execution.

Katharine—Henry VIII IV.ii

Urns and odours bring away;
Vapours, sighs, darken the day;
Our dole more deadly looks than dying—
Balms and gums and heavy cheers,
Sacred vials fill'd with tears,
And clamours through the wild air flying.

Come, all sad and solemn shows
That are quick-eyed Pleasure's foes;
We convent naught else but woes.
We convent naught else but woes.   *Queens—TNK I.v*

This world's a city full of straying streets,
And death's the market-place where each one meets.

3rd Queen—TNK I.v

MUSIC: "Touches of sweet harmony"

For Orpheus' lute was strung with poets' sinews,
Whose golden touch could soften steel and stones,

Make tigers tame and huge leviathans
Forsake unsounded deeps to dance on sands.

Proteus—TGV III.ii

How irksome is this music to my heart!
When such strings jar, what hope of harmony?

King—2 Henry VI II.i

Then music with her silver sound
With speedy help doth lend redress.   *Peter—RJ IV.v*

How sweet the moonlight sleeps upon this bank!
Here will we sit and let the sounds of music
Creep in our ears: soft stillness and the night
Become the touches of sweet harmony.   *Lorenzo—MV V.i*

The man that hath no music in himself,
Nor is not mov'd with concord of sweet sounds,
Is fit for treason, stratagems and spoils;
The motions of his spirit are dull as night
And his affections dark as Erebus;
Let no such man be trusted.   *Lorenzo—MV V.i*

If music be the food of love, play on;
Give me excess of it, that, surfeiting,
The appetite may sicken, and so die.
That strain again! It had a dying fall:
O, it came o'er my ear like the sweet sound,
That breathes upon a bank of violets,
Stealing and giving odour!   *Orsino—TN I.i*

Music oft hath such a charm
To make bad good, and good provoke to harm.
Duke—MforM IV.i

Give me some music; music, moody food
Of us that trade in love.   *Cleopatra—A&C II.v*

Hark, hark! the lark at heaven's gate sings,
    And Phoebus 'gins arise,
His steeds to water at those springs
    On challic'd flow'rs that lies;
And winking Mary-buds begin
    To open their golden eyes:
With every thing that pretty is,
    My lady sweet, arise:
        Arise, arise.   *Musicians—Cymbeline II.iii*

If this penetrate, I will consider your music the better: if it
do not, it is a vice in her ears, which horse-hairs and calves'-
guts, nor the voice of unpaved eunuch to boot, can never
amend.   *Cloten—Cymbeline II.iii*

Where should this music be? i' th' air or th' earth?
It sounds no more; and, sure, it waits upon
Some god o' th' island. Sitting on a bank,
Weeping again the king my father's wrack,
This music crept by me upon the waters,
Allaying both their fury and my passion
With its sweet air.   *Ferdinand—Tempest I.ii*

Be not afeard; the isle is full of noises,
Sounds and sweet airs, that give delight and hurt not.
Sometimes a thousand twangling instruments

Will hum about mine ears, and sometimes voices
That, if I then had wak'd after long sleep,
Will make me sleep again: and then, in dreaming,
The clouds methought would open and show riches
Ready to drop upon me, that, when I wak'd,
I cried to dream again.   *Caliban—Tempest III.ii*

Orpheus with his lute made trees,
And the mountain tops that freeze,
    Bow themselves when he did sing:
To his music plants and flowers
Ever sprung; as sun and showers
    There had made a lasting spring.

Every thing that heard him play,
Even the billows of the sea,
    Hung their heads, and then lay by.
In such sweet music is such art,
Killing care and grief of heart
    Fall asleep, or hearing, die.   *Women—Henry VIII III.i*

N

NAME: "What's in a name?"

O, be some other name!
What's in a name? that which we call a rose
By any other name would smell as sweet.   *Juliet—RJ II.ii*

In what vile part of this anatomy
Doth my name lodge? tell me that I may sack
The hateful mansion.   *Romeo—RJ III.iii*

My life thou shalt command, but not my shame:
The one my duty owes; but my fair name,
Despite of death that lives upon my grave,
To dark dishonour's use thou shalt not have.
                                Mowbray—Richard II I.i

The purest treasure mortal times afford
Is spotless reputation: that away,
Men are gilded loam or painted clay.
                                Mowbray—Richard II I.i

Is not the king's name twenty thousand names?
Arm, arm, my name!   *King Richard—Richard II III.ii*

O that I were as great
As is my grief, or lesser than my name!
                        King Richard—Richard II III.ii

I would to God thou and I knew where a commodity of good names were to be bought.   *Falstaff—1 Henry IV I.ii*

I would to God my name were not so terrible to the enemy as it is: I were better to be eaten to death with a rust than to be scoured to nothing with perpetual motion.
                              Falstaff—2 Henry IV I.ii

I have a whole school of tongues in this belly of mine, and not a tongue of them all speaks any other word but my name.   *Falstaff—2 Henry IV IV.iii*

What a wounded name,
Things standing thus unknown, shall live behind me!
If thou didst ever hold me in thy heart,
Absent thee from felicity awhile,
And in this harsh world draw thy breath in pain,
To tell my story.   *Hamlet—Hamlet V.ii*

Reputation, reputation, reputation! O, I have lost my reputation! I have lost the immortal part of myself and what remains is bestial.   *Cassio—Othello II.iii*

Reputation is an idle and most false imposition; oft got without merit, and lost without deserving:
                              Iago—Othello II.iii

Good name in man and woman, dear my lord,
Is the immediate jewel of their souls:
Who steals my purse steals trash; 'tis something, nothing;
'Twas mine, 'tis his, and has been slave to thousands;
But he that filches from me my good name
Robs me of that which not enriches him
And makes me poor indeed.   *Iago—Othello III.iii*

I have offended reputation,
A most ignoble swerving.   *Antony—A&C III.xi*

NATURE: "Common mother, thou"

When the sun shines let foolish gnats make sport,
But creep in crannies when he hides his beams.
                              Antipholus of Syracuse—CE II.ii

The current that with gentle murmur glides,
Thou knowst, being stopped, impatiently doth rage;
But when his fair course is not hindered,
He makes sweet music with the enameled stones,
Giving a gentle kiss to every sedge
He overtaketh in his pilgrimage,
And so by many winding nooks he strays,
With willing sport, to the wild ocean.   *Julia—TGV II.vii*

How use doth breed a habit in a man!
This shadowy desert, unfrequented woods,
I better brook than flourishing peopled towns;
Here can I sit alone, unseen of any,
And to the nightingale's complaining notes
Tune my distresses and record my woes.
                                    Valentine—TGV V.iv

I know a bank where the wild thyme blows,
Where oxlips and the nodding violet grows,
Quite over-canopied with luscious woodbine,
With sweet-musk-roses and with eglantine.
                                    Oberon—MND II.i

Dark night, that from the eye his function takes,
The ear more quick of apprehension makes;
Wherein it doth impair the seeing sense,
It pays the hearing double recompense.

Hermia—MND III.ii

Now the hungry lion roars,
    And the wolf behowls the moon;
Whilst the heavy ploughman snores,
    All with weary task fordone.
Now the wasted brands do glow,
    Whilst the screech-owl, screeching loud,
Puts the wretch that lies in woe
    In remembrance of a shroud.   *Puck—MND V.i*

See how the morning opes her golden gates,
And takes her farewell of the glorious sun!
How well resembles it the prime of youth,
Trimm'd like a younker prancing to his love!

Richard—3 Henry VI II.i

Gives not the hawthorn-bush a sweeter shade
To shepherds looking on their silly sheep,
Than doth a rich embroider'd canopy
To kings that fear their subjects' treachery?

King—3 Henry VI II.v

Ill blows the wind that profits nobody.

Son—3 Henry VI II.v

A little fire is quickly trodden out;
Which, being suffer'd, rivers cannot quench.

Clarence—3 Henry VI IV.viii

For every cloud engenders not a storm.
                              Clarence—3 Henry VI V.iii

Our aery buildeth in the cedar's top,
And dallies with the wind and scorns the sun.
                              Richard—Richard III I.iii

Small herbs have grace; great weeds do grow apace.
                              York—Richard III II.iv

The weary sun hath made a golden set,
And, by the bright tract of his fiery car,
Gives token of a goodly day tomorrow.
                              Richmond—Richard III V.iii

The birds chant melody on every bush,
The snake lies rolled in the cheerful sun,
The green leaves quiver with the cooling wind
And make a chequer'd shadow on the ground.
                              Tamora—Titus II.iii

When heaven doth weep, doth not the earth o'erflow?
If the winds rage, doth not the sea wax mad,
Threat'ning the welkin with his big-swoln face?
                              Titus—Titus III.i

O, mickle is the powerful grace that lies
In plants, herbs, stones, and their true qualities:
For nought so vile that on the earth doth live
But to the earth some special good doth give,
Nor aught so good but strain'd from that fair use
Revolts from true birth, stumbling on abuse:
Virtue itself turns vice, being misapplied;

And vice sometime by action dignified.
Within the infant rind of this weak flower
Poison hath residence and medicine power:
For this, being smelt, with that part cheers each part;
Being tasted, slays all senses with the heart.
Two such opposed kings encamp them still
In man as well as herbs, grace and rude will;
And where the worser is predominant,
Full soon the canker death eats up the plant.

Friar Laurence—RJ II.iii

The moon shines bright: in such a night as this,
When the sweet wind did gently kiss the trees
And they did make no noise, in such a night
Troilus methinks mounted the Troyan walls
And sigh'd his soul toward the Grecian tents,
Where Cressid lay that night.   *Lorenzo—MV V.i*

The pleasant'st angling is to see the fish
Cut with her golden oars the silver stream,
And greedily devour the treacherous bait.

Ursula—Much Ado III.i

Now, my co-mates and brothers in exile,
Hath not old custom made this life more sweet
Than that of painted pomp? Are not these woods
More free from peril than the envious court?
Here feel we not the penalty of Adam,
The seasons' difference, as the icy fang
And churlish chiding of the winter's wind,
Which, when it bites and blows upon my body,
Even till I shrink with cold, I smile and say
'This is no flattery: these are counselors

That feelingly persuade me what I am.'
Sweet are the uses of adversity,
Which, like the toad, ugly and venomous,
Wears yet a precious jewel in his head;
And this our life exempt from public haunt,
Finds tongues in trees, books in the running brooks,
Sermons in stones and good in every thing.

Duke Senior—AYLI II.i

Under the greenwood tree,
Who loves to lie with me,
And turn his merry note
Unto the sweet bird's throat,
Come hither, come hither, come hither:
Here shall he see
No enemy
But winter and rough weather.

Who doth ambition shun
And loves to live i' the sun,
Seeking the food he eats
And pleas'd with what he gets,
Come hither, come hither, come hither:
Here shall he see
No enemy
But winter and rough weather.   *Amiens—AYLI II.v*

Since the more fair and crystal is the sky,
The uglier seem the clouds that in it fly.

Bolingbroke—Richard II I.i

Small show'rs last long, but sudden storms are short.

John of Gaunt—Richard II II.i

The bay-trees in our country are all wither'd
And meteors fright the fixed stars of heaven;
The pale-fac'd moon looks bloody on the earth
And lean-look'd prophets whisper fearful change;
Rich men look sad and ruffians dance and leap,
The one in fear to lose what they enjoy,
The other to enjoy by rage and war:
These signs forerun the death or fall of kings
Captain—Richard II II.iv

The sun sets weeping in the lowly west,
Witnessing storms to come, woe and unrest.
Salisbury—Richard II. II.iv

Know'st thou not
That when the searching eye of heaven is hid,
Behind the globe, that lights the lower world,
Then thieves and robbers range abroad unseen
In murders and in outrage, boldly here;
But when from under this terrestrial ball
He fires the proud tops of the eastern pines
And darts his light through every guilty hole,
Then murders, treasons and detested sins,
The cloak of night being pluck'd from off their backs,
Stand bare and naked trembling at themselves?
King Richard—Richard II III.ii

If the young dace be a bait for the old pike, I see no reason
in the law of nature but I may snap at him.
Falstaff—2 Henry IV III.iii

The strawberry grows underneath the nettle
And wholesome berries thrive and ripen best
Neighbour'd by fruit of baser quality.
Archbishop of Ely—Henry V I.i

I have seen tempests, when the scolding winds
Have riv'd the knotty oaks, and I have seen
Th' ambitious ocean swell and rage and foam,
To be exalted with the threat'ning clouds:
But never till to-night, never till now,
Did I go through a tempest dropping fire.
Either there is a civil strife in heaven,
Or else the world, too saucy with the gods,
Incenses them to send destruction.   *Casca—JC I.iii*

The dragon wing of night o'erspreads the earth.
                                   Achilles—TC V.viii

But, look, the morn, in russet mantle clad,
Walks o'er the dew of yon high eastward hill.
                                   Horatio—Hamlet I.i

There's rosemary, that's for remembrance; pray you, love,
remember: and there's pansies, that's for thoughts.
                                   Ophelia—Hamlet IV.v

There's fennel for you, and columbines: there's rue for you;
and here's some for me: we may call it herb of grace o'
Sundays. O, you must wear your rue with a difference.
                                   Ophelia—Hamlet IV.v

For nature so preposterously to err,
Being not deficient, blind, or lame of sense,
Sans witchcraft could not.   *Brabantio—Othello I.iii*

Thou, Nature, art my goddess; to thy law
My services are bound.   *Edmund—Lear I.ii*

Blow, winds, and crack your cheeks! rage! blow!
You cataracts and hurricanoes, spout

Till you have drench'd our steeples, drown'd the cocks!
You sulph'rous and thought-executing fires,
Vaunt-couriers of oak-cleaving thunderbolts,
Singe my white head! And thou, all-shaking thunder,
Strike flat the thick rotundity o' th' world!
Crack nature's moulds, all germens spill at once,
That makes ingrateful man!   *Lear—Lear III.ii*

              Since I was man,
Such sheets of fire, such bursts of horrid thunder,
Such groans of roaring wind and rain, I never
Remember to have heard: man's nature cannot carry
Th' affliction nor the fear.   *Kent—Lear III.ii*

The tyranny of the open night's too rough
For nature to endure.   *Kent—Lear III.iv*

            Common mother, thou,
Whose womb unmeasurable, and infinite breast,
Teems, and feeds all; whose self-same mettle,
Whereof thy proud child, arrogant man, is puff'd,
Engenders the black toad and adder blue,
The gilded newt and eyeless venom'd worm,
With all th' abhorred births below crisp heaven
Whereon Hyperion's quick'ning fire doth shine;
Yield him, who all thy human sons doth hate,
From forth thy precious bosom, one poor root!
                     Timon—Timon IV.iii

         Behold, the earth hath roots;
Within this mile break forth a hundred springs;
The oaks bear mast, the briers scarlet hips;
The bounteous housewife, nature, on each bush
Lays her full mess before you.   *Timon—Timon IV.iii*

Now o'er the one half-world
Nature seems dead, and wicked dreams abuse
The curtain'd sleep; witchcraft celebrates
Pale Hecate's offerings, and wither'd murder,
Alarum'd by his sentinel, the wolf,
Whose howl's his watch, thus with his stealthy pace,
With Tarquin's ravishing strides, towards his design
Moves like a ghost.   *Macbeth—Macbeth II.i*

Thou see'st, the heavens, as troubled with man's act,
Threatens his bloody stage: by th' clock, 'tis day,
And yet dark night strangles the traveling lamp:
Is't night's predominance, or the day's shame,
That darkness does the face of earth entomb,
When living light should kiss it?   *Ross—Macbeth II.iv*

                    Come, seeling night,
Scarf up the tender eye of pitiful day;
And with thy bloody and invisible hand
Cancel and tear to pieces that great bond
Which keeps me pale!   *Macbeth—Macbeth III.ii*

Sometime we see a cloud that's dragonish;
A vapour sometime like a bear or lion,
A tower'd citadel, a pendent rock,
A forked mountain, or blue promontory
With trees upon 't, that nod unto the world,
And mock our eyes with air: thou hast seen these signs;
They are black vesper's pageants.   *Antony—A&C IV.xiv*

    How hard it is to hide the sparks of nature!
                    Belarius—Cymbeline III.iii

We marry
A gentler scion to the wildest stock,
And make conceive a bark of baser kind
By bud of nobler race: this is an art
Which does mend nature, change it rather, but
The art itself is nature.   *Polixenes—WT IV.iv*

Here's flow'rs for you;
Hot lavender, mints, savory, marjoram;
The marigold, that goes to bed wi' th' sun
And with him rises weeping: these are flow'rs
Of middle summer, and I think they are given
To men of middle age.   *Perdita—WT IV.iv*

The sky, it seems, would pour down stinking pitch,
But that the sea, mounting to th' welkin's cheek,
Dashes the fire out.   *Miranda—Tempest I.ii*

Full fathom five thy father lies;
        Of his bones are coral made;
Those are pearls that were his eyes:
        Nothing of him that doth fade
But doth suffer a sea-change
Into something rich and strange.
Sea-nymphs hourly ring his knell.   *Ariel—Tempest I.ii*

I prithee, let me bring thee where crabs grow;
And I with my long nails will dig thee pig-nuts;
Show thee a jay's nest and instruct thee how
To snare the nimble marmoset; I'll bring thee
To clust'ring filberts and sometimes I'll get thee
Young scamels from the rock.   *Caliban—Tempest II.ii*

Where the bee sucks, there suck I:
In a cowslip's bell I lie;
There I couch when owls do cry
On the bat's back I do fly
After summer merrily.
Merrily, merrily shall I live now
Under the blossom that hangs on the bough.

Ariel—Tempest V.i

Roses, their sharp spines being gone,
Not royal in their smells alone
But in their hue;
Maiden pinks of odour faint,
Daisies smell-less yet most quaint,
And sweet thyme true;

Primrose, first-born child of Ver,
Merry springtime's harbinger,
With harebells dim,
Oxlips in their cradles growing,
Marigolds on death beds blowing,
Lark's-heels trim:

All dear Nature's children sweet
Lie 'fore bride and bridegroom's feet,
Blessing their sense.
Not an angel of the air,
Bird melodious, or bird fair,
Is absent hence.

The crow, the sland'rous cuckoo, nor
The boding raven, nor chough hoar,
Nor chatt'ring pie,

May on our bridge-house perch or sing,
Or with them any discord bring,
But from it fly.   *Boy—TNK I.i*

        But the whole week's not fair
If any day it rain.   *Palamon—TNK III.i*

P

PHILOSOPHY: " Thought is free"

Who by repentance is not satisfied
Is nor of heaven nor earth, for these are pleas'd.
By penitence th' Eternal's wrath's appeased:

Valentine—TGV V.iv

Methinks the truth should live from age to age,
As 'twere retail'd to all posterity,
Even to the general all-ending day.

Prince Edward—Richard III III.i

To be possess'd with double pomp,
To guard a title that was rich before,
To gild refined gold, to paint the lily,
To throw a perfume on the violet,
To smooth the ice, or add another hue
Unto the rainbow, or with taper-light
To seek the beauteous eye of heaven to garnish,
Is wasteful and ridiculous excess. *Salisbury—King John IV.ii*

Some men there are love not a gaping pig;
Some, that are mad if they behold a cat;
And others, when the bagpipe sings i' th' nose,
Cannot contain their urine; for affection,
Mistress of passion, sways it to the mood
Of what it likes or loathes. *Shylock—MV IV.i*

How far that little candle throws his beams!
So shines a good deed in a naughty world.   *Portia—MV V.i*

For there was never yet philosopher
That could endure the toothache patiently.

Leonato—Much Ado V.i

I know the more one sickens the worse at ease he is; and
that he that wants money, means and content is without
three good friends; that the property of rain is to wet and
fire to burn; that good pasture makes fat sheep, and that a
great cause of the night is lack of the sun; that he that hath
learned no wit by nature nor art may complain of good
breeding or comes of a very dull kindred.

Corin—AYLI III.ii

Things sweet to taste prove in digestion sour.

John of Gaunt—Richard II I.iii

O, who can hold a fire in his hand
By thinking on the frosty Caucasus?
Or cloy the hungry edge of appetite
By bare imagination of a feast?
Or wallow naked in December snow
By thinking on fantastic summer's heat?
O, no! the apprehension of the good
Gives but the greater feeling to the worse:
Fell sorrow's tooth doth never rankle more
Than when he bites, but lanceth not the sore.

Bolingbroke—Richard II I.iii

Wisdom cries out in the streets, and no man regards it.

Prince—1 Henry IV I.ii

He that of greatest works is finisher
Oft does them by the weakest minister:
So holy writ in babes hath judgement shown,
When judges have been babes; great floods have flown
From simple sources, and great seas have dried
When miracles have by the great'st been denied.

Helena—All's Well II.i

Inspired merit so by breath is barr'd:
It is not so with Him that all things knows
As 'tis with us that square our guess by shows;
But most it is presumption in us when
The help of heaven we count the act of men.

Helena—All's Well II.i

They say miracles are past; and we have our philosophical
persons, to make modern and familiar, things supernatural
and causeless. Hence is it that we make trifles of terrors, en-
sconcing ourselves into seeming knowledge, when we should
submit ourselves to an unknown fear.

Lafeu—All's Well II.iii

Praising what is lost
Makes the remembrance dear.   *King—All's Well V.iii*

But love that comes too late,
Like a remorseful pardon slowly carried,
To the great sender turns a sour offence,
Crying, 'That's good that's gone.' Our rash faults
Make trivial price of serious things we have,
Not knowing them until we know their grave.

King—All's Well V.iii

As surfeit is the father of much fast,
So every scope by the immoderate use
Turns to restraint. Our natures do pursue,
Like rats that ravin down their proper bane,
A thirsty evil, and when we drink we die.

Claudio—MforM I.ii

In the reproof of chance
Lies the true proof of men; the sea being smooth,
How many shallow bauble boats dare sail
Upon her patient breast, making their way
With those of nobler bulk!   *Nestor—TC I.iii*

A mote it is to trouble the mind's eye.

Horatio—Hamlet I.i

There are more things in heaven and earth, Horatio,
Than are dreamt of in your philosophy. *Hamlet—Hamlet I.v*

What a piece of work is a man! how noble in reason! how
infinite in faculties! in form and moving how express and
admirable! in action how like an angel! in apprehension
how like a god! the beauty of the world! the paragon of an-
imals! And yet, to me, what is this quintessence of dust?
man delights not me; no, nor woman neither.

Hamlet—Hamlet II.ii

'Sblood, there is something in this more than natural, if philosophy could find it out.   *Hamlet—Hamlet II.ii*

Our indiscretion sometime serves us well,
When our deep plots do pall; and that should learn us
There's a divinity that shapes our ends,
Rough-hew them how we will.   *Hamlet—Hamlet V.ii*

'Tis dangerous when the baser nature comes
Between the pass and fell incensed points
Of mighty opposites.   *Hamlet—Hamlet V.ii*

We defy augury: there's a special providence in the fall of a
sparrow. If it be now; 'tis not to come; if it be not to come, it
will be now; if it be not now, yet it will come; the readiness
is all: since no man of aught he leaves knows, what is 't to
leave betimes? Let be.   *Hamlet—Hamlet V.ii*

When remedies are past, the griefs are ended
By seeing the worst, which late on hopes depended.
To mourn a mischief that is past and gone
Is the next way to draw new mischief on.
What cannot be preserv'd when fortune takes,
Patience her injury a mock'ry makes.
The robb'd that smiles steals something from the thief;
He robs himself that spends a bootless grief.
                                        Duke—Othello I.iii

I should be wise, for honesty's a fool
And loses that it works for.   *Iago—Othello III.iii*

Nothing will come of nothing.
                                        Lear—Lear I.i

O, reason not the need! Our basest beggars
Are in the poorest thing superfluous:
Allow not nature more than nature needs,
Man's life is cheap as beast's: thou art a lady;
If only to go warm were gorgeous,
Why, nature needs not what thou gorgeous wear'st,
Which scarcely keeps thee warm. But, for true need,—
You heavens, give me that patience, patience I need!
                                        Lear—Lear II.iv

> When the mind's free
> The body's delicate: the tempest in my mind
> Doth from my senses take all feeling else
> Save what beats there.   *Lear—Lear III.iv*

Is man no more than this? Consider him well. Thou owest the worm no silk, the beast no hide, the sheep no wool, the cat no perfume. Ha! here's three on's are sophisticated! Thou art the thing itself: unaccommodated man is no more but such a poor, bare, forked animal as thou art.

Lear—Lear III.iv

> When we our betters see bearing our woes,
> We scarcely think our miseries our foes.
> Who alone suffers suffers most i' the mind,
> Leaving free things and happy shows behind;
> But then the mind much sufferance doth o'erskip,
> When grief hath mates, and bearing fellowship.
>   *Edgar—Lear III.vi*

> Yet better thus, and known to be contemn'd,
> Than still contemn'd and flatter'd. To be worst,
> The lowest and most dejected thing of fortune,
> Stands still in esperance, lives not in fear:
> The lamentable change is from the best;
> The worst returns to laughter.   *Edgar—Lear IV.i*

> The worst is not
> So long as we can say 'This is the worst.'   *Edgar—Lear IV.i*

> As flies to wanton boys, are we to th' gods,
> They kill us for their sport.   *Gloucester—Lear IV.i*

Thou must be patient; we came crying hither:
Thou know'st, the first time we smell the air,
We wawl and cry.   *Lear—Lear IV.vi*

To-morrow, and to-morrow, and to-morrow,
Creeps in this petty pace from day to day
To the last syllable of recorded time,
And all our yesterdays have lighted fools
The way to dusty death. Out, out, brief candle!
Life's but a walking shadow, a poor player
That struts and frets his hour upon the stage
And then is heard no more: it is a tale
Told by an idiot, full of sound and fury,
Signifying nothing.   *Macbeth—Macbeth V.v*

The loyalty well held to fools does make
Our faith mere folly: yet he that can endure
To follow with allegiance a fall'n lord
Does conquer him that did his master conquer,
And earns a place in the story.   *Enobarbus—A&C III.xiii*

          When valour preys on reason,
It eats the sword it fights with.   *Enobarbus—A&C III.xiii*

All love the womb that their first being bred,
Then give my tongue like leave to love my head.
                              Pericles—Pericles I.i

          The passions of the mind,
That have their first conception by mis-dread,
Have after-nourishment and life by care;
And what was first but fear what might be done,
Grows elder now and cares it be not done.
                              Pericles—Pericles I.ii

Opinion's but a fool, that makes us scan
The outward habit by the inward man.
Simonides—Pericles II.ii

Virtue and cunning were endowments greater
Than nobleness and riches: careless heirs
May the two latter darken and expend;
But immortality attends the former,
Making a man a god.   *Cerimon—Pericles III.ii*

Blessed be those,
How mean soe'er, that have their honest wills,
Which seasons comfort.   *Imogen—Cymbeline I.vi*

The cloyed will,
That satiate yet unsatisfied desire, that tub
Both fill'd and running, ravening first the lamb
Longs after for the garbage.   *Iachimo—Cymbeline I.vi*

O, this life
Is nobler than attending for a check,
Richer than doing nothing for a bauble,
Prouder than rustling in unpaid-for silk:
Such gain the cap of him that makes him fine,
Yet keeps his book uncross'd: no life to ours.
Belarius—Cymbeline III.iii

Weariness
Can snore upon the flint, when resty sloth
Finds the down pillow hard.   *Belarius—Cymbeline III.vi*

Triumphs for nothing and lamenting toys
Is jollity for apes and grief for boys.
Guiderius—Cymbeline IV.ii

Every good servant does not all commands:
No bond but to do just ones.   *Posthumus—Cymbeline V.i*

If pow'rs divine
Behold our human actions, as they do,
I doubt not then but innocence shall make
False accusation blush and tyranny
Tremble at patience.   *Hermione—WT III.ii*

But as th' unthought-on accident is guilty
To what we wildly do, so we profess
Ourselves to be the slaves of chance and flies
Of every wind that blows.   *Camillo—WT IV.iv*

                    Ebbing men, indeed,
Most often do so near the bottom run
By their own fear or sloth.   *Antonio—Tempest II.i*

There be some sports are painful, and their labour
Delight in them sets off: some kinds of baseness
Are nobly undergone and most poor matters
Point to rich ends.   *Ferdinand—Tempest III.i*

Flout 'em and scout 'em
And scout 'em and flout 'em;
            Thought is free.   *Stephano—Tempest III.i*

How beauteous mankind is! O brave new world,
That has such people in 't!   *Miranda—Tempest V.i*

                    Verily,
I swear, 'tis better to be lowly born,
And range with humble livers in content,
Than to be perk'd up in a glist'ring grief,
And wear a golden sorrow.   *Anne—Henry VIII II.iii*

THE PROFESSIONS: "Spare none but such as go in clouted shoon"

Pirates may make cheap pennyworths of their pillage
And purchase friends and give to courtezans,
Still reveling like lords till all be gone;
While as the silly owner of the goods
Weeps over them and wrings his hapless hands
And shakes his head and trembling stands aloof,
While all is shar'd and all is borne away,
Ready to starve and dare not touch his own.

York—2 Henry VI I.i

O miserable age! virtue is not regarded in handicrafts-men.

Bevis—2 Henry VI IV.ii

The first thing we do, let's kill all the lawyers.

Dick—2 Henry VI IV.ii

We will not leave one lord, one gentleman:
Spare none but such as go in clouted shoon;
For they are thrifty honest men and such
As would, but that they dare not, take our parts.

Cade—2 Henry VI IV.ii

When workmen strive to do better than well,
They do confound their skill in covetousness;
And oftentimes excusing of a fault
Doth make the fault the worse by the excuse,
As patches set upon a little breach
Discredit more in hiding of the fault
Than did the fault before it was so patch'd.

Pembroke—King John IV.ii

It is written, that the shoemaker should meddle with his yard, and the tailor with his last, the fisher with his pencil, and the painter with his nets.   *Servant—RJ I.ii*

A tapster is a good trade; an old cloak makes a new jerkin; a withered serving-man a fresh tapster.

Falstaff—Merry Wives I.iii

O, how full of briers is this working-day world!

Rosalind—AYLI I.iii

O good old man, how well in thee appears
The constant service of the antique world,
When service sweat for duty, not for meed!
Thou art not for the fashion of these times,
Where none will sweat but for promotion,
And having that, do choke their service up
Even with the having.   *Orlando—AYLI II.ii*

Alas, poor duke! the task he undertakes
Is numbr'ing sands and drinking oceans dry.

Green—Richard II II.ii

'Tis no sin for a man to labour in his vocation.

Falstaff—1 Henry IV I.ii

I am joined with no foot landrakers, no long-staff sixpenny strikers, none of these mad mustachio purple-hued malt-worms; but with nobility and tranquility, burgomasters and great oneyers, such as can hold in, such as will strike sooner than speak, and speak sooner than drink, and drink sooner than pray: and yet, zounds, I lie; for they pray continually to their saint, the commonwealth; or rather, not pray to her,

but prey on her, for they ride up and down on her and make
her their boots.   *Gadshill—1 Henry IV II.i*

      Therefore doth heaven divide
The state of man in divers functions,
Setting endeavour in continual motion;
To which is fixed, as an aim or butt,
Obedience: for so work the honey-bees,
Creatures that by a rule in nature teach
The act of order to a peopled kingdom.
They have a king and officers of sorts;
Where some, like magistrates, correct at home,
Others, like merchants, venture trade abroad,
Others, like soldiers, armed in their stings,
Make boot upon the summer's velvet buds,
Which pillage they with merry march bring home
To the tent-royal of their emperor;
Who, busied in his majesty, surveys
The singing masons building roofs of gold,
The civil citizens kneading up the honey,
The poor mechanic porters crowding in
Their heavy burdens at his narrow gate,
The sad-eyed justice, with his surly hum,
Delivering o'er to executors pale
The lazy yawning drone. I this infer,
That many things, having full reference
To one consent, may work contrariously:
As many arrows, loosed several ways,
Come to one mark; as many ways meet in one town;
As many fresh streams meet in one salt sea;
As many lines close in the dial's centre;
So may a thousand actions, once afoot,
End in one purpose, and be all well borne
Without defeat.   *Archbishop of Canterbury—Henry V I.ii*

Is this a holiday? what! know you not,
Being mechanical, you ought not walk
Upon a labouring day without the sign
Of your profession?   *Flavius—JC I.i*

Truly, sir, all that I live by is with the awl: I meddle with no
tradesman's matters, nor women's matters; but withal I am,
indeed, sir, a surgeon to old shoes; when they are in great
danger, I recover them. As proper men as ever trod upon
neat's leather have gone upon my handiwork.
                                    Second Commoner—JC I.i

O world! world! world! thus is the poor agent despised! O
traitors and bawds, how earnestly are you set a-work, and
how ill requited! why should our endeavour be so loved
and the performance so loathed?   *Pandarus—TC V.x*

There is no ancient gentlemen but gardeners, ditchers, and
grave-makers: they hold up Adam's profession.
                                    First Clown—Hamlet V.i

I'll speak a prophecy ere I go:
        When priests are more in word than matter:
        When brewers mar their malt with water;
        When nobles are their tailors' tutors;
        No heretics burn'd, but wenches' suitors;
        When every case in law is right;
        No squire in debt, nor no poor knight;
        When slanders do not live in tongues;
        Nor cutpurses come not to throngs;
        When usurers tell their gold i' th' field;
        And bawds and whores do churches build;
        Then shall the realm of Albion
        Come to great confusion.   *Fool—Lear III.ii*

                Trust not the physician;
His antidotes are poison, and he slays
More than you rob: take wealth and lives together;
Do villany, do, since you protest to do't,
Like workmen.

                                 Timon—Timon IV.iii

Here is more matter for a hot brain: every lane's end, every
shop, church, session, hanging, yields a careful man work.

                                 Autolycus—WT IV.iv

R

REASON: "That noble and most sovereign reason"

Who will not change a raven for a dove?
The will of man is by his reason sway'd;
And reason says you are the worthier maid.
Things growing are not ripe until their season;
So I, being young, till now ripe not to reason;
And touching now the point of human skill,
Reason becomes the marshal to my will
And leads me to your eyes, where I o'erlook
Love's stories written in love's richest book.

Lysander—MND II.ii

You fur your gloves with reason.

Troilus—TC II.ii

Nay, if we talk of reason,
Let's shut our gates and sleep: manhood and honour
Should have hare-hearts, would they but fat their thoughts
With this cramm'd reason: reason and respect
Make livers pale and lustihood deject.   *Troilus—TC II.ii*

Blind fear, that seeing reason leads, finds safer footing than
blind reason stumbling without fear; to fear the worst oft
cures the worse.   *Cressida—TC III.ii*

O God! a beast that wants discourse of reason
Would have mourned longer.   *Hamlet—Hamlet I.ii*

Now see that noble and most sovereign reason,
Like sweet bells jangled, out of time and harsh.
                                   Ophelia—Hamlet III.i

If the balance of our lives had not one scale of reason to
poise another of sensuality, the blood and baseness of our
natures would conduct us to most preposterous conclu-
sions: but we have reason to cool our raging motions, our
carnal stings, our unbitted lusts.   *Iago—Othello I.iii*

Who can be wise, amaz'd, temp'rate and furious,
Loyal and neutral, in a moment? No man:
Th' expedition of my violent love
Outrun the pauser, reason.   *Macbeth—Macbeth II.iii*

Though with their high wrongs I am struck to th' quick,
Yet with my nobler reason 'gainst my fury
Do I take part: the rarer action is
In virtue than in vengeance.   *Prospero—Tempest V.i*

    Let your reason with your choler question
What 'tis you go about: to climb steep hills
Requires slow pace at first: anger is like
A full-hot horse, who being allow'd his way,
Self-mettle fires him.   *Norfolk—Henry VIII I.i*

    Our reasons are not prophets
When oft our fancies are.   *Emilia—TNK V.iii*

S

SEASONS: "The seasons change their manners"

The spring is near when green geese are a-feeding.
Berowne—LLL I.i

At Christmas I no more desire a rose
Than wish a snow in May's new-fangled shows;
But like of each thing that in season grows.
Berowne—LLL I.i

O, how this spring of love resembleth
  The uncertain glory of an April day,
Which now shows all the beauty of the sun,
  And by and by a cloud takes all away.   *Proteus—TGV I.iii*

Winter tames man, woman, and beast.
Curtis—TS IV.i

Thus sometimes hath the brightest day a cloud;
And after summer evermore succeeds
Barren winter, with his wrathful nipping cold:
So cares and joys abound, as seasons fleet.
Gloucester—2 Henry VI II.iv

When clouds are seen, wise men put on their cloaks;
When great leaves fall, then winter is at hand;

When the sun sets, who doth not look for night?
Untimely storms makes men expect a dearth.
                    Third Citizen—Richard III II.iii

Short summers lightly have a forward spring.
                    Richard—Richard III III.i

How like a winter hath my absence been
From thee, the pleasure of the fleeting year!
What freezings have I felt, what dark days seen!
What old December's bareness everywhere!
And yet this time removed was summer's time,
The teeming autumn big with rich increase,
Bearing the wanton burthen of the prime,
Like widowed wombs after their lords' decrease:
Yet this abundant issue seemed to me
But hope of orphans, and unfathered fruit,
For summer and his pleasures wait on thee,
And thou away, the very birds are mute.
     Or if they sing, 'tis with so dull a cheer,
     That leaves look pale, dreading the winter's near.
                    Sonnet 97

From you have I been absent in the spring,
When proud-pied April (dressed in all his trim)
Hath put a spirit of youth in every thing,
That heavy Saturn laughed and leaped with him.
Yet nor the lays of birds, nor the sweet smell
Of different flowers in odour and in hue,
Could make me any summer's story tell,
Or from their proud lap pluck them where they grew:
Nor did I wonder at the lily's white,
Nor praise the deep vermilion in the rose,

They were but sweet, but figures of delight:
Drawn after you, you pattern of all those.
　　Yet seemed it winter still, and you away
　　As with your shadow I with these did play.　　*Sonnet 98*

How many things by season season'd are
To their right praise and true perfection!　　*Portia—MV V.i*

Why, this is like the mending of highways
In summer, where the ways are fair enough.
　　　　　　　　　　　　　　Gratiano—MV V.i

　　　　　Why, what's the matter,
That you have such a February face,
So full of frost, of storm and cloudiness?
　　　　　　　　　Don Pedro—Much Ado V.iv

Blow, blow, thou winter wind,
　　Thou art not so unkind
　　　As man's ingratitude;
　　Thy tooth is not so keen,
　　Because thou art not seen,
　　　Although thy breath be rude.
Heigh-ho! sing, heigh-ho! unto the green holly:
Most friendship is feigning, most loving mere folly:
　　Then, heigh-ho, the holly!
　　　This life is most jolly.

　　Freeze, freeze, thou bitter sky,
　　That dost not bite so nigh
　　　As benefits forgot:
　　Though thou the waters warp,
　　Thy sting is not so sharp
　　　As friend rememb'red not.

Heigh-ho! sing, heigh-ho! unto the green holly:
Most friendship is feigning, most loving mere folly.
    Then heigh-ho, the holly!
       This life is most jolly.   *Amiens—AYLI II.vii*

It was a lover and his lass,
    With a hey, and a ho, and a hey nonino,
That o'er the green corn-field did pass
    In the spring time, the only pretty ring time,
When birds do sing, hey ding a ding, ding:
Sweet lovers love the spring.

Between the acres of the rye,
    With a hey, and a ho, and a hey nonino,
These pretty country folk would lie,
    In spring time, the only pretty ring time,
When birds do sing, hey ding a ding, ding:
Sweet lovers love the spring.

This carol they began that hour,
    With a hey, and a ho, and a hey nonino,
How that a life was but a flower,
    In spring time, the only pretty ring time,
When birds do sing, hey ding a ding, ding:
Sweet lovers love the spring.

And therefore take the present time
    With a hey, and a ho, and a hey nonino,
For love is crowned with the prime
    In spring time, the only pretty ring time,
When birds do sing, hey ding a ding, ding:
Sweet lovers love the spring.
       First & Second Pages—AYLI V.iii

Why, this is very midsummer madness.
Olivia—TN III.iv

More matter for a May morning.
Fabian—TN III.iv

The seasons change their manners, as the year
Had found some months asleep and leap'd them over.
Gloucester—2 Henry IV IV.iv

Some say that ever 'gainst that season comes
Wherein our Saviour's birth is celebrated,
The bird of dawning singeth all night long:
And then, they say, no spirit dare stir abroad;
The nights are wholesome; then no planets strike,
No fairy takes, nor witch hath power to charm,
So hallow'd and so gracious is that time.
Marcellus—Hamlet I.i

Tomorrow is Saint Valentine's Day,
    All in the morning betime,
And I a maid at your window,
    To be your Valentine.
Then up he rose, and donn'd his clothes,
    And dupp'd the chamber door;
Let in the maid, that out a maid
    Never departed more.   *Ophelia—Hamlet IV.v*

Winter's not gone yet, if the wild-geese fly that way.
Fool—Lear II.iv

The April's in her eyes: it is love's spring,
And these the showers to bring it on.   *Antony—A&C III.ii*

He makes a July's day short as December.

Polixenes—WT I.ii

A sad tale's best for winter.

Mamilius—WT II.i

When daffodils begin to peer,
  With heigh! the doxy over the dale,
Why, then comes in the sweet o' the year;
  For the red blood reigns in the winter's pale.

The white sheet bleaching on the hedge,
  With heigh! the sweet birds, O, how they sing!
Doth set my pugging tooth on edge;
  For a quart of ale is a dish for a king.

The lark, that tirra-lyra chants,
  With heigh! with heigh! the thrush and the jay,
Are summer songs for me and my aunts,
  While we lie tumbling in the hay.

But shall I go mourn for that, my dear?
  The pale moon shines by night:
And when I wander here and there,
  I then do most go right.

If tinkers may have leave to live,
  And bear the sow-skin budget,
Then my account I well may give,
  And in the stocks avouch it.   *Autolycus—WT IV.iii*

          Sir, the year growing ancient,
Not yet on summer's death; nor on the birth

Of trembling winter, the fairest flow'rs o' th' season
Are our carnations and streak'd gillyvors,
Which some call nature's bastards.   *Perdita—WT IV.iv*

SELFHOOD: "Who is it can tell me who I am?"

I to the world am like a drop of water
That in the ocean seeks another drop,
Who, falling there to find his fellow forth,
Unseen, inquisitive, confounds himself.
                              Antipholus of Syracuse—CE I.ii

I am an ass, I am a woman's man and besides myself.
                              Dromio of Syracuse—CE III.ii

My thoughts are whirled like a potter's wheel;
I know not where I am, nor what I do.
                              Talbot—1 Henry VI I.v

I do protest I never lov'd myself
Till now infixed I beheld myself
Drawn in the flattering table of her eye.
                              Lewis—King John II.i

Tut, I have lost myself; I am not here.
                              Romeo—RJ I.i

When in disgrace with Fortune and men's eyes
I all alone beweep my outcast state,
And trouble deaf heaven with my bootless cries,
And look upon my self and curse my fate,
Wishing me like to one more rich in hope,

Featured like him, like him with friends possessed,
Desiring this man's art, and that man's scope,
With what I most enjoy contented least,
Yet in these thoughts my self almost despising,
Haply I think on thee, and then my state
(Like to the lark at break of day arising
From sullen earth) sings hymns at heaven's gate,
　　For thy sweet love remembered such wealth brings,
　　That then I scorn to change my state with kings.

Sonnet 29

And such a want-wit sadness makes of me,
That I have much ado to know myself.　　*Antonio—MV I.i*

He knows me as the blind man knows the cuckoo,
By the bad voice.　　　　　　　　　　*Portia—MV V.i*

　　I'll rather be unmannerly than troublesome.

Slender—Merry Wives I.i

By the very fangs of malice I swear, I am not that I play.

Viola—TN I.v

Now my foes tell me plainly I am an ass; so that by my foes,
sir, I profit in the knowledge of myself, and by my friends I
am abused.　　　　　　　　　　　　　*Feste—TN V.i*

Be that thou know'st thou art, and then thou art
As great as that thou fear'st.　　　*Olivia—TN V.i*

　　　　　　　　I am sworn brother, sweet,
To grim Necessity, and he and I
Will keep a league till death.　　*King Richard—Richard II V.i*

Before I knew thee, Hal, I knew nothing; and now am I, if a
man should speak truly, little better than one of the wicked.

Falstaff—1 Henry IV I.ii

I know you all, and will awhile uphold
The unyok'd humour of your idleness:
Yet herein will I imitate the sun,
Who doth permit the base contagious clouds
To smother up his beauty from the world,
That when he please again to be himself,
Being wanted, he may be more wond'red at,
By breaking through the foul and ugly mists
Of vapours that did seem to strangle him.
If all the year were playing holidays,
To sport would be as tedious as to work;
But when they seldom come, they wish'd for come,
And nothing pleaseth but rare accidents.
So, when this loose behaviour I throw off
And pay the debt I never promised,
By how much better than my word I am,
By so much shall I falsify men's hopes;
And like bright metal on a sullen ground,
My reformation, glitt'ring o'er my fault,
Shall show more goodly and attract more eyes
Than that which hath no foil to set it off.
I'll so offend, to make offence a skill;
Redeeming time when men think least I will.

Prince—1 Henry IV I.ii

The tide of blood in me
Hath proudly flow'd in vanity till now;
Now doth it turn and ebb back to the sea,
Where it shall mingle with the state of floods
And flow henceforth in formal majesty.

King Henry V—2 Henry IV V.ii

Presume not that I am the thing I was;
For God doth know, so shall the world perceive,
That I have turn'd away my former self;
So will I those that kept me company.
King Henry V—2 Henry IV V.v

If I could pray to move, prayers would move me:
But I am constant as the northern star,
Of whose true-fix'd and resting quality
There is no fellow in the firmament.   *Caesar—JC III.i*

Simply the thing I am
Shall make me live. Who knows himself a braggart,
Let him fear this, for it will come to pass
That every braggart shall be found an ass.
Parolles—All's Well IV.iii

I have a kind of self resides with you;
But an unkind self, that itself will leave,
To be another's fool.   *Cressida—TC III.ii*

Fear not my truth: the moral of my wit
Is 'plain and true'; there's all the reach of it.
Troilus—IV.iv

I am myself indifferent honest; but yet I could accuse me of
such things that it were better my mother had not borne
me: I am very proud, revengeful, ambitious, with more offen-
ces at my beck than I have thoughts to put them in, imagination to give them shape, or time to act them in. What
should such fellows as I do crawling between earth and
heaven? We are arrant knaves, all; believe none of us.
Hamlet—Hamlet III.i

Lord, we know what we are, but know not what we may be.

Ophelia—Hamlet IV.v

I pray you, in your letters,
When you shall these unlucky deeds relate,
Speak of me as I am; nothing extenuate,
Nor set down aught in malice: then must you speak
Of one that lov'd not wisely but too well;
Of one not easily jealous, but being wrought
Perplex'd in the extreme; of one whose hand,
Like the base Judean, threw a pearl away
Richer than all his tribe; of one whose subdu'd eyes,
Albeit unused to the melting mood,
Drop tears as fast as the Arabian trees
Their medicinal gum   *Othello—Othello V.ii*

I do profess to be no less than I seem; to serve him truly that
will put me in trust; to love him that is honest; to converse
with him that is wise, and says little; to fear judgement; to
fight when I cannot choose; and to eat no fish.

Kent—Lear I.iv

Poor naked wretches, wheresoe'er you are,
That bide the pelting of this pitiless storm,
How shall your houseless heads and unfed sides,
Your loop'd and window'd raggedness, defend you
From seasons such as these? O, I have ta'en
Too little care of this! Take physic, pomp;
Expose thyself to feel what wretches feel,
That thou mayst shake the superflux to them,
And show the heavens more just.   *Lear—Lear III.iv*

Immortal gods, I crave no pelf;
I pray for no man but myself;

Grant I may never prove so fond,
To trust man on his oath or bond;
Or a harlot, for her weeping;
Or a dog, that seems a-sleeping;
Or a keeper with my freedom;
Or my friends, if I should need 'em.
Amen. So fall to 't:
Rich men sin, and I eat root.   *Apemantus—Timon I.ii*

To know my deed, 'twere best not know myself.
                              Macbeth—Macbeth II.ii

                    I had else been perfect,
Whole as the marble, founded as the rock,
As broad and general as the casing air;
But now I am cabin'd, cribb'd, confin'd, bound in
To saucy doubts and fears.   *Macbeth—Macbeth III.iv*

I have liv'd long enough: my way of life
Is fall'n into the sear, the yellow leaf;
And that which should accompany old age,
As honour, love, obedience, troops of friends,
I must not look to have; but, in their stead,
Curses, not loud but deep, mouth-honour, breath,
Which the poor heart would fain deny, and dare not.
                              Macbeth—Macbeth V.iii

I have fled myself; and have instructed cowards
To run and show their shoulders.   *Antony—A&C III.xi*

I am known to be a humourous patrician, and one that
loves a cup of hot wine with not a drop of allaying Tiber in
't; said to be something imperfect in favouring the first
complaint; hasty and tinder-like upon too trivial motion;

one that converses more with the buttock of the night than
with the forehead of the morning: what I think I utter, and
spend my malice in my breath.   *Menenius—Coriolanus II.i*

Anger's my meat; I sup upon myself,
And so shall starve with feeding.
                              Volumnia—Coriolanus IV.ii

             I'll never
Be such a gosling to obey instinct, but stand,
As if a man were author of himself
And knew no other kin.   *Coriolanus—Coriolanus V.iii*

What I have been I have forgot to know;
But what I am, want teaches me to think on.
                              Pericles—Pericles II.i

I am but sorry, not afeard; delay'd,
But nothing alt'red: what I was, I am;
More straining on for plucking back, not following
My leash unwillingly.   *Florizel—WT IV.iv*

           Brief, I am,
To those that prate and have done, no companion;
To those that boast and have not, a defier;
To those that would and cannot, a rejoicer.
                              Palamon—TNK V.i

SELF-SLAUGHTER: "To be or not to be"

       I do find it cowardly and vile,
For fear of what might fall, so to prevent
The time of life: *Brutus—JC V.i*

O, that this too too sullied flesh would melt,
Thaw and resolve itself into a dew!
Or that the Everlasting had not fix'd
His canon 'gainst self-slaughter! O God! God!
How weary, stale, flat and unprofitable
Seem to me all the uses of this world!
Fie on 't! ah fie! 'tis an unweeded garden,
That grows to seed; things rank and gross in nature
Possess it merely.   *Hamlet—Hamlet I.ii*

To be, or not to be: that is the question:
Whether 'tis nobler in the mind to suffer
The slings and arrows of outrageous fortune,
Or to take arms against a sea of troubles,
And by opposing end them? To die: to sleep;
No more; and by a sleep to say we end
The heartache and the thousand natural shocks
That flesh is heir to, 'tis a consummation
Devoutly to be wish'd. To die, to sleep;
To sleep: perchance to dream: ay, there's the rub;
For in that sleep of death what dreams may come
When we have shuffled off this mortal coil,
Must give us pause: there's the respect
That makes calamity of so long life;
For who would bear the whips and scorns of time,
Th' oppressor's wrong, the proud man's contumely,
The pangs of despis'd love, the law's delay,
The insolence of office and the spurns
That patient merit of th' unworthy takes,
When he himself might his quietus make
With a bare bodkin? who would fardels bear,
To grunt and sweat under a weary life,
But that the dread of something after death,

The undiscover'd country from whose bourn
No traveller returns, puzzles the will
And makes us rather bear those ills we have
Than fly to others that we know not of?
Thus conscience does make cowards of us all;
And thus the native hue of resolution
Is sicklied o'er with the pale cast of thought,
And enterprises of great pitch and moment
With this regard their currents turn awry,
And lose the name of action.   *Hamlet—Hamlet III.i*

I will incontinently drown myself.
                    Roderigo—Othello I.iii

Come, be a man. Drown thyself! drown cats and blind puppies.   *Iago—Othello I.iii*

O you mighty gods!
This world I do renounce, and, in your sights,
Shake patiently my great affliction off:
                    Gloucester—Lear IV.vi

You ever-gentle gods, take my breath from me;
Let not my worser spirit tempt me again
To die before you please!   *Gloucester—Lear IV.vi*

I will go seek
Some ditch wherein to die; the foul'st best fits
My latter part of life.   *Enobarbus—A&C IV.vi*

O sovereign mistress of true melancholy,
The poisonous damp of night disponge upon me,
That life, a very rebel to my will,
May hang no longer on me.   *Enobarbus—A&C IV.ix*

                    Then is it sin
To rush into the secret house of death,
Ere death dare come to us?   *Cleopatra—A&C IV.xv*

Give me my robe, put on my crown; I have
Immortal longings in me: now no more
The juice of Egypt's grape shall moist this lip:
Yare, yare, good Iras; quick. Methinks I hear
Antony call; I see him rouse himself
To praise my noble act; I hear him mock
The luck of Caesar, which the gods give men
To excuse their after wrath: husband, I come:
Now to that name my courage prove my title!
I am fire and air; my other elements
I give to baser life.   *Cleopatra—A&C V.ii*

                 Against self-slaughter
There is a prohibition so divine
That cravens my weak hand.   *Imogen—Cymbeline III.iv*

SLEEP: "The death of each day's life"

Care keeps his watch in every old man's eye,
And where care lodges, sleep will never lie;
But where unbruised youth with unstuff'd brain
Doth couch his limbs, there golden sleep doth reign.
                    Friar Laurence—RJ II.iii

Is it thy will, thy image should keep open
My heavy eyelids to the weary night?
Dost thou desire my slumbers should be broken,
While shadows like to thee do mock my sight?
Is it thy spirit that thou send'st from thee

So far from home into my deeds to pry,
To find out shames and idle hours in me,
The scope and tenure of thy jealousy?
O no, thy love, though much, is not so great,
It is my love that keeps mine eye awake,
To play the watchman ever for thy sake.
    For thee watch I, whilst thou dost wake elsewhere,
    From me far off, with others all too near.   *Sonnet 61*

To be up after midnight and to go to bed then, is early: so
that to go to bed after midnight is to go to bed betimes.
                                            Sir Toby—TN II.iii

Canst thou, O partial sleep, give thy repose
To the wet sea-boy in an hour so rude,
And in the calmest and most stillest night,
With all appliances and means to boot,
Deny it to a king? Then happy low, lie down!
Uneasy lies the head that wears a crown.
                                    King—2 Henry IV III.i

Enjoy the honey-heavy dew of slumber:
Thou hast no figures nor no fantasies,
Which busy care draws in the brains of men;
Therefore thou sleep'st so sound.   *Brutus—JC II.i*

            Not poppy, nor mandragora,
Nor all the drowsy syrups of the world,
Shall ever medicine thee to that sweet sleep
Which thou owedst yesterday.   *Iago—Othello III.iii*

Sleep shall neither night nor day
Hang upon his pent-house lid
He shall live a man forbid:

Weary sev'nights nine times nine
Shall he dwindle, peak and pine.　*First Witch—Macbeth I.iii*

Methought I heard a voice cry 'Sleep no more!
Macbeth does murder sleep,' the innocent sleep,
Sleep that knits up the ravell'd sleave of care,
The death of each day's life, sore labour's bath,
Balm of hurt minds, great nature's second course,
Chief nourisher in life's feast.　　*Macbeth—Macbeth II.ii*

Yet I have known those which have walked in their sleep
who have died holily in their beds.　*Doctor—Macbeth V.i*

Unnatural deeds
Do breed unnatural troubles; infected minds
To their deaf pillows will discharge their secrets:
More needs she the divine than the physician.
Doctor—Macbeth V.i

O sleep, thou ape of death!
Iachimo—Cymbeline II.ii

Since I receiv'd command to do this business
I have not slept one wink.　*Pisanio—Cymbeline III.iv*

He that sleeps feels not the toothache.
First Gaoler—Cymbeline V.iv

SPEECH AND LANGUAGE: "Wild and whirling words"

They have been at a great feast of languages, and stolen the
scraps.　　　*Moth—LLL V.i*

A heavy heart bears not a humble tongue.
Princess—LLL V.ii

His speech was like a tangled chain; nothing impaired, but all disordered.
Theseus—MND V.i

Speak on; but be not over-tedious.
Burgundy—1 Henry VI III.iii

An honest tale speeds best being plainly told.
Queen Elizabeth—Richard III IV.iv

Here's a large mouth, indeed,
That spits forth death and mountains, rocks and seas,
Talks as familiarly of roaring lions
As maids of thirteen do of puppy-dogs!
What cannoneer begot this lusty blood?
He speaks plain cannon fire, and smoke and bounce;
He gives the bastinado with his tongue:
Our ears are cudgell'd; not one word of his
But buffets better than a fist of France:
Zounds! I was never so bethump'd with words
Since I first call'd my brother's father dad.
Bastard—King John II.i

Silence is only commendable
In a neat's tongue dried and a maid not vendible.
Gratiano—MV I.i

How every fool can play upon the word! I think the best grace of wit will shortly turn into silence, and discourse grow commendable in none only but parrots.
Launcelot—MV III.v

Thou wilt be like a lover presently
And tire the hearer with a book of words.
Don Pedro—Much Ado I.i

Silence is the perfectest herald of joy!
Claudio—Much Ado II.i

Foul words is but foul wind, and foul wind is but foul
breath, and foul breath is noisome.
Beatrice—Much Ado V.ii

Very good orators, when they are out, they will spit; and for
lovers lacking—God warn us!—matter, the cleanliest shift
is to kiss.
Rosalind—AYLI IV.i

What great ones do the less will prattle of.
Captain—TN I.ii

They call drinking deep, dyeing scarlet; and when you
breathe in your watering, they cry 'hem!' and bid you play
it off. To conclude, I am so good a proficient in one quarter
of an hour, that I can drink with any tinker in his own language during my life.   *Prince Hal—1 Henry IV II.iv*

Rumour is a pipe
Blown by surmises, jealousies, conjectures,
And of so easy and so plain a stop
That the blunt monster with uncounted heads,
The still-discordant wav'ring multitude,
Can play upon it.   *Rumour—2 Henry IV I.i*

Yet the first bringer of unwelcome news
Hath but a losing office, and his tongue

Sounds ever after as a sullen bell,
Rememb'red tolling a departed friend.
                    Northumberland—2 Henry IV I.i

A captain! God's light, these villians will make the word as
odious as the word 'occupy,' which was an excellent good
word before it was ill sorted: therefore captains had need
look to't.   *Doll—2 Henry IV II.iv*

Rumour doth double, like the voice and echo,
The numbers of the fear'd.   *Warwick—2 Henry IV III.i*

                    In her youth
There is a prone and speechless dialect,
Such as move men; beside, she hath prosperous art
When she will play with reason and discourse,
And well she can persuade.   *Claudio—MforM I.ii*

Those that understood him smiled at one another and shook
their heads; but, for mine own part, it was Greek to me.
                    Casca—JC I.ii

That in the captain's but a choleric word,
Which in the soldier is flat blasphemy. *Isabella—MforM II.ii*

                    What king so strong
Can tie the gall up in the slanderous tongue?
                    Duke—MforM III.ii

He'll answer nobody; he professes not answering: speaking
is for beggars; he wears his tongue in's arms.
                    Thersites—TC III.iii

Words, words, mere words, no matter from the heart.
                    Troilus—TC V.iii

These are but wild and whirling words, my lord.
Horatio—Hamlet I.v

A knavish speech sleeps in a foolish ear.
Hamlet—Hamlet IV.ii

But words are words; I never yet did hear
That the bruis'd heart was pierced through the ear.
Brabantio—Othello I.iii

From this time forth I never will speak word.
Iago—Othello V.ii

I know, sir, I am no flatterer: he that beguiled you in a plain
accent was a plain knave.   *Kent—Lear II.ii*

The weight of this sad time we must obey;
Speak what we feel, not what we ought to say.
Edgar—Lear V.iii

Though it be honest, it is never good
To bring bad news; give to a gracious message
An host of tongues; but let ill tidings tell
Themselves when they be felt.   *Cleopatra—A&C II.v*

You cram these words into mine ears against
The stomach of my sense.   *Alonso—Tempest II.i*

The truth you speak doth lack some gentleness
And time to speak it in: you rub the sore,
When you should bring the plaster.   *Gonzalo—Tempest II.i*

He has
Strangled his language in his tears.   *King—Henry VIII V.i*

SUSPICION: "What damned minutes"

Who finds the heifer dead and bleeding fresh
And sees fast by a butcher with an axe,
But will suspect 'twas he that made the slaughter?

Warwick—2 Henry VI III.ii

Suspicion always haunts the guilty mind,
The thief doth fear each bush an officer.

Gloucester—3 Henry VI V.vi

See what a ready tongue suspicion hath!
He that but fears the thing he would not know
Hath by instinct knowledge from others' eyes
That what he fear'd is chanced.   *2 Henry IV I.i*

If I suspect without cause, why then make sport at me; then
let me be your jest; I deserve it.   *Ford—Merry Wives III.iii*

Let me have men about me that are fat;
Sleek-headed men and such as sleep o' nights:
Yond Cassius has a lean and hungry look;
He thinks too much; such men are dangerous.

Caesar—JC I.ii

O, beware, my lord, of jealousy:
It is the green-ey'd monster which doth mock
The meat it feeds on: that cuckold lives in bliss
Who, certain of his fate, loves not his wronger;
But, O, what damned minutes tells he o'er
Who dotes, yet doubts, suspects, yet strongly loves!

Iago—Othello III.iii

Think'st thou I'ld make a life of jealousy,
To follow still the changes of the moon
With fresh suspicions? No; to be once in doubt
Is once to be resolv'd: *Othello—Othello III.iii*

             Trifles light as air
Are to the jealous confirmations strong
As proofs of holy writ.   *Iago—Othello III.iii*

             Guiltiness will speak
Though tongues were out of use.   *Iago—Othello V.i*

T

THEATRE: "All the world's a stage"

As an unperfect actor on the stage,
Who with his fear is put beside his part,
Or some fierce thing replete with too much rage,
Whose strength's abundance weakens his own heart;
So I, for fear of trust, forget to say
The perfect ceremony of love's right.   *Sonnet 23 1–6*

To bring in—God shield us—a lion among ladies, is a most dreadful thing, for there is not a more fearful wild-fowl than your lion living, and we ought to look to it.
                                        Bottom—MND III.i

Why, I can smile, and murder whiles I smile,
And cry 'Content' to that which grieves my heart,
And wet my cheeks with artificial tears,
And frame my face to all occasions.
                            Gloucester—3 Henry VI III.ii

Tut, I can counterfeit the deep tragedian;
Speak and look back, and pry on every side,
Tremble and start at wagging of a straw,
Intending deep suspicion: ghastly looks
Are at my service, like enforced smiles;
And both are ready in their offices,
At any time, to grave my stratagems.
                            Buckingham—R III III.v

I hold the world but as the world, Gratiano;
A stage where every man must play a part,
And mine a sad one.   *Antonio—MV I.i*

This wide and universal theatre
Presents more woeful pageants than the scene
Wherein we play in.   *Duke Senior—AYLI II.vii*

                    All the world's a stage,
And all the men and women merely players:
They have their exits and their entrances;
And one man in his time plays many parts,
His acts being seven ages. At first the infant,
Mewling and puking in the nurse's arms,
And then the whining school-boy, with his satchel
And shining morning face, creeping like snail
Unwillingly to school. And then the lover,
Sighing like furnace, with a woeful ballad
Made to his mistress' eyebrow. Then a soldier,
Full of strange oaths and bearded like the pard,
Jealous in honour, sudden and quick in quarrel,
Seeking the bubble reputation
Even in the cannon's mouth. And then the justice,
In fair round belly with good capon lin'd,
With eyes severe and beard of formal cut,
Full of wise saws and modern instances;
And so he plays his part. The sixth age shifts
Into the lean and slipper'd pantaloon,
With spectacles on nose and pouch on side,
His youthful hose, well sav'd, a world too wide,
For his shrunk shank; and his big manly voice,
Turning again toward childish treble, pipes
And whistles in his sound. Last scene of all,

That ends this strange eventful history,
Is second childishness and mere oblivion,
Sans teeth, sans eyes, sans taste, sans everything.

Jacques—AYLI II.vii

In a theatre, the eyes of men,
After a well-grac'd actor leaves the stage,
Are idly bent on him that enters next,
Thinking his prattle to be tedious.   *York—Richard II V.ii*

O for a Muse of fire, that would ascend
The brightest heaven of invention,
A kingdom for a stage, princes to act
And monarchs to behold the swelling scene!

Chorus—Henry V I.i

Good my lord, will you see the players well bestowed? Do
you hear, let them be well used; for they are the abstract and
brief chronicles of the time.   *Hamlet—Hamlet II.ii*

Speak the speech I pray you, as I pronounced it to you, trip-
pingly on the tongue: but if you mouth it, as many of your
players do, I had as lief the towncrier spoke my lines. Nor
do not saw the air too much with your hand, thus, but use
all gently; for in the very torrent, tempest, and, as I may say,
whirlwind of your passion, you must acquire and beget a
temperance that may give it smoothness. O, it offends me to
the soul to hear a robustious periwig-pated fellow tear a
passion to tatters, to very rags, to split the ears of the
groundlings, who for the most part are capable of nothing
but inexplicable dumbshows and noise: I would have such
a fellow whipped for o'er-doing Termagant; it out-herods
Herod: pray you, avoid it.   *Hamlet—III.ii*

Be not too tame neither, but let your own discretion be your tutor: suit the action to the word, the word to the action; with this special observance, that you o'er-step not the modesty of nature: for any thing so overdone is from the purpose of playing, whose end, both at the first and now, was and is, to hold, as 't were, the mirror up to nature; to show virtue her own feature, scorn her own image, and the very age and body of the time his form and pressure. Now this overdone, or come tardy off, though it make the unskilful laugh, cannot but make the judicious grieve; the censure of the which one must in your allowance o'erweigh a whole theatre of others. O, there be players that I have seen play, and heard others praise, and that highly, not to speak it profanely, that, neither having the accent of Christians nor the gait of Christian, pagan, nor man, have so strutted and bellowed that I have thought some of nature's journeymen had made men and not made them well, they imitated humanity so abominably.   *Hamlet—Hamlet III.ii*

And let those that play your clowns speak no more than is set down for them; for there be of them that will themselves laugh, to set on some quantity of barren spectators to laugh too, though in the mean time, some necessary question of the play be then to be considered: that's villanous, and shows a most pitiful ambition in the fool that uses it.
                    Hamlet—Hamlet III.ii

O, what a rogue and peasant slave am I!
Is it not monstrous that this player here,
But in a fiction, in a dream of passion,
Could force his soul so to his own conceit
That from her working all his visage wann'd,
Tears in his eyes, distraction in 's aspect,
A broken voice, and his whole function suiting
With forms to his conceit? and all for nothing!
                    Hamlet—Hamlet II.ii

Our revels now are ended. These our actors,
As I foretold you, were all spirits and
Are melted into air, into thin air:
And, like the baseless fabric of this vision,
The cloud-capp'd tow'rs, the gorgeous palaces,
The solemn temples, the great globe itself,
Yea, all which it inherit, shall dissolve
And, like this insubstantial pageant faded,
Leave not a rack behind. We are such stuff
As dreams are made on, and our little life
Is rounded with a sleep.   *Prospero—Tempest IV.i*

TIME: "The chimes at midnight"

Time is a very bankrupt and owes more than he's worth to
      season.
Nay, he's a thief too, have you not heard men say,
That Time comes stealing on by night and day?
                          Dromio of Syracuse—CE IV.ii

Time is the nurse and breeder of all good.
                          Proteus—TGV III.i

When I do count the clock that tells the time,
And see the brave day sunk in hideous night,
When I behold the violet past prime,
And sable curls all silvered o'er with white:
When lofty trees I see barren of leaves,
Which erst from heat did canopy the herd
And summer's green all girded up in sheaves
Borne on the bier with white and bristly beard:
Then of thy beauty do I question make
That thou among the wastes of time must go,
Since sweets and beauties do themselves forsake,

And die as fast as they see others grow,
    And nothing 'gainst Time's scythe can make defence
    Save breed to brave him, when he takes thee hence.

Sonnet 12

Devouring Time, blunt thou the lion's paws,
And make the earth devour her own sweet brood,
Pluck the keen teeth from the fierce tiger's jaws,
And burn the long-lived phoenix in her blood,
Make glad and sorry seasons as thou fleet'st,
And do what'er thou wilt, swift-footed Time,
To the wide world and all her fading sweets:
But I forbid thee one most heinous crime,
O carve not with thy hours my love's fair brow,
Nor draw no lines there with thine antique pen,
Him in thy course untainted do allow,
For beauty's pattern to succeeding men.
        Yet do thy worst, old Time: despite thy wrong,
        My love shall in my verse ever live young.   *Sonnet 19*

Like as the waves make towards the pebbled shore,
So do our minutes hasten to their end,
Each changing place with that which goes before,
In sequent toil all forwards do contend.
Nativity, once in the main of light,
Crawls to maturity, wherewith being crowned,
Crooked eclipses 'gainst his glory fight,
And Time that gave, doth now his gift confound.
Time doth transfix the flourish set on youth,
And delves the parallels in beauty's brow,
Feeds on the rarities of nature's truth,
And nothing stands but for his scythe to mow.
        And yet to times in hope, my verse shall stand
        Praising thy worth, despite his cruel hand.   *Sonnet 60*

I wasted time, and now doth time waste me;
For now hath time made me his numb'ring clock
My thoughts are minutes; and with sighs they jar
Their watches on unto mine eyes, the outward watch,
Whereto my finger, like a dial's point,
Is pointing still, in cleansing them from tears.

King Richard—Richard II V.v

What a devil hast thou to do with the time of the day?
Unless hours were cups of sack and minutes capons and
clocks the tongues of bawds and dials the signs of leaping-
houses and the blessed sun himself a fair hot wench in
flame-coloured taffeta, I see no reason why thou shouldst
be so superfluous to demand the time of the day.

Prince—1 Henry IV I.ii

O gentlemen, the time of life is short!
To spend that shortness basely were too long,
If life did ride upon a dial's point,
Still ending at the arrival of an hour.

Hotspur—1 Henry IV V.ii

Thus we play the fools with the time, and the spirits
of the wise sit in the clouds and mock us.

Prince—2 Henry IV II.ii

There is a history in all men's lives,
Figuring the nature of the times deceas'd;
The which observ'd, a man may prophesy,
With a near aim, of the main chance of things
As yet not come to life, which in their seeds
And weak beginnings lie intreasured.
Such things become the hatch and brood of time.

Warwick—2 Henry IV III.i

We have heard the chimes at midnight.
Falstaff—2 Henry IV III.ii

Now he weighs time
Even to the utmost grain.   *Exeter—Henry V II.iv*

There is a tide in the affairs of men,
Which, taken at the flood, leads on to fortune;
Omitted, all the voyage of their life
Is bound in shallows and in miseries.   *Brutus—JC IV.iii*

For Time is like a fashionable host
That slightly shakes his parting guest by th' hand,
And with his arms outstretch'd, as he would fly,
Grasps in the comer: the welcome ever smiles,
And farewell goes out sighing. Let not virtue seek
Remuneration for the thing it was;
For beauty, wit,
High birth, vigour of bone, desert in service,
Love, friendship, charity, are subjects all
To envious and calumniating Time.   *Ulysses—TC III.iii*

The end crowns all,
And that old common arbitrator, Time,
Will one day end it.   *Hector—TC IV.v*

The time is out of joint.
Hamlet—Hamlet I.v

There are many events in the womb of time which will be
delivered.   *Iago—Othello I.iii*

Time shall unfold what plighted cunning hides:
Who covers faults, at last shame them derides.
Cordelia—Lear I.i

We have seen the best of our time: machinations, hollow-
ness, treachery, and all ruinous disorders follow us disqui-
etly to our graves.   *Gloucester—Lear I.ii*

Come what come may,
Time and the hour runs through the roughest day.
                                   Macbeth—Macbeth I.iii

Every time
Serves for the matter that is then born in 't.
                                   Enobarbus—A&C II.ii

Whereby I see that Time's the king of men,
He's both their parent, and he is their grave,
And gives them what he will, not what they crave.
                                   Pericles—Pericles II.iii

I, that please some, try all, both joy and terror
Of good and bad, that makes and unfolds error,
Now take upon me, in the name of Time,
To use my wings.   *Time—WT IV.i*

V

VIRTUE: "Virtue is bold"

> He lives in fame that died in virtue's cause.
> *All—Titus I.i*

> Is it a world to hide virtues in?
> *Sir Toby—TN I.iii*

Dost thou think, because thou art virtuous, there shall be no
more cakes and ale? *Sir Toby—TN II.iii*

From lowest place when virtuous things proceed,
The place is dignified by th' doer's deed:
Where great additions swell's, and virtue none,
It is a dropsied honour. Good alone
Is good without a name *King—All's Well II.iii*

The web of our life is of a mingled yarn, good and ill together; our virtues would be proud, if our faults whipped
them not; and our crimes would despair, if they were not
cherished by our virtues. *First Lord—All's Well IV.iii*

> Virtue is bold, and goodness never fearful.
> *Duke—MforM III.i*

But virtue, as it never will be moved,
Though lewdness court it in a shape of heaven,

So lost, though to a radiant angel link'd,
Will sate itself in a celestial bed,
And prey on garbage.   *Ghost—Hamlet I.v*

VOWS: "Men's faiths are wafer-cakes"

It is great sin to swear unto a sin,
But greater sin to keep a sinful oath.
Who can be bound by any solemn vow
To do a murd'rous deed, to rob a man,
To force a spotless virgin's chastity,
To reave the orphan of his patrimony,
To wrong the widow from her custom'd right,
And have no other reason for this wrong
But that he was bound by a solemn oath?
                    Salisbury—2 Henry VI V.i

An oath is of no moment, being not took
Before a true and lawful magistrate,
That hath authority over him that swears.
                    Richard—3 Henry VI I.ii

For trust not him that hath once broken faith.
                    Queen—3 Henry VI IV.iv

An idiot holds his bauble for a god
And keeps the oath which by that god he swears.
                    Aaron—Titus V.i

The oath of a lover is no stronger than the word of a tapster;
they are both the confirmer of false reckonings.
                    Celia—AYLI III.iv

What other oath
Than honesty to honesty engag'd.
That this shall be, or we will fall for it?
Swear priests and cowards and men cautelous,
Old feeble carrions and such suffering souls
That welcome wrongs; unto bad causes swear
Such creatures as men doubt; but do not stain
The even virtue of our enterprise,
Nor th' insuppressive mettle of our spirits,
To think that or our cause or our performance
Did need an oath.   *Brutus—JC II.i*

Trust none;
For oaths are straws, men's faiths are wafer-cakes,
And hold-fast is the only dog, my duck.
                              Pistol—Henry V II.iii

It is the purpose that makes strong the vow;
But vows to every purpose must not hold.
                              Cassandra—TC V.iii

Ay, springes to catch woodcocks. I do know,
When the blood burns, how prodigal the soul
Lends the tongue vows.   *Polonius—Hamlet I.iii*

Men's vows are women's traitors
                         Imogen—Cymbeline III.iv

The strongest oaths are straw
To th' fire i' th' blood.   *Prospero—Tempest IV.i*

W

WAR: "Thou son of hell"

O war, thou son of hell,
Whom angry heavens do make their minister,
Throw in the frozen bosoms of our part
Hot coals of vengeance! Let no soldier fly.
Young Clifford—2 Henry VI V.ii

So triumph thieves upon their conquer'd booty;
So true men yield, with robbers so o'ermatched.
York—3 Henry VI I.iv

The harder match'd, the greater victory.
King Edward—3 Henry VI V.i

The tiger now hath seiz'd the gentle hind;
Insulting tyranny begins to jut
Upon the innocent and aweless throne:
Welcome, destruction, death, and massacre!
Queen Elizabeth—Richard III II.iv

Then, if you fight against God's enemy,
God will in justice ward you as his soldiers;
If you do sweat to put a tyrant down,
You sleep in peace, the tyrant being slain.
Richmond—Richard III V.iii

We must awake endeavour for defence;
For courage mounteth with occasion.

Austria—King John II.i

O, now doth Death line his dead chaps with steel;
The swords of soldiers are his teeth, his fangs;
And now he feasts, mousing the flesh of men,
In undetermin'd differences of kings.

Bastard—King John II.i

Now powers from home and discontents at home
Meet in one line; and vast confusion waits,
As doth a raven on a sick-fall'n beast,
The imminent decay of wrested pomp.

Bastard—King John IV.iii

I'll broach the tadpole on my rapier's point.

Demetrius—Titus IV.ii

A victory is twice itself when the achiever brings home full
numbers.   Leonato—Much Ado I.i

To fear the foe, since fear oppresseth strength,
Gives in your weakness strength unto your foe,
And so your follies fight against yourself.
Fear, and be slain; no worse can come to fight:
And fight and die is death destroying death;
Where fearing dying pays death servile breath.

Carlisle—Richard II III.ii

This is no world
To play with mammets and to tilt with lips:
We must have bloody noses and crack'd crowns,
And pass them current too.   Hotspur—1 Henry IV II.iii

Tut, tut; good enough to toss; food for powder, food for powder; they'll fill a pit as well as better: tush, man, mortal men, mortal men.   *Falstaff—1 Henry IV IV.ii*

For that same word, rebellion, did divide
The action of their bodies from their souls;
And they did fight with queasiness, constrain'd,
As men drink potions, that their weapons only
Seem'd on our side; but, for their spirits and souls,
This word, rebellion, it had froze them up,
As fish are in a pond.   *Morton—2 Henry IV I.i*

A peace is of the nature of a conquest;
For then both parties nobly are subdu'd,
And neither party loser.   *Archbishop—2 Henry IV IV.ii*

I dare not fight; but I will wink and hold out mine iron: it is a simple one; but what though? it will toast cheese, and it will endure cold as another man's sword will: and there's an end.   *Corporal Nym—Henry V II.i*

Once more unto the breach, dear friends, once more;
Or close the wall up with our English dead.
In peace there's nothing so becomes a man
As modest stillness and humility:
But when the blast of war blows in our ears,
Then imitate the action of the tiger;
Stiffen the sinews, summon up the blood,
Disguise fair nature with hard-favour'd rage;
Then lend the eye a terrible aspect;
Let it pry through the portage of the head
Like the brass cannon; let the brow o'erwhelm it
As fearfully as doth a galled rock
O'erhang and jutty his confounded base,

Swill'd with the wild and wasteful ocean.
Now set the teeth and stretch the nostril wide,
Hold hard the breath and bend up every spirit
To his full height. On, on, you noblest English,
Whose blood is fet from fathers of war-proof!
Fathers that, like so many Alexanders,
Have in these parts from morn till even fought
And sheath'd their swords for lack of argument:
Dishonour not your mothers; now attest
That those whom you call'd fathers did beget you,
Be copy now to men of grosser blood,
And teach them how to war. And you, good yeomen,
Whose limbs were made in England, show us here
The mettle of your pasture; let us swear
That you are worth your breeding; which I doubt not;
For there is none of you so mean and base,
That hath not noble luster in your eyes
I see you stand like greyhounds in the slips,
Straining upon the start. The game's afoot:
Follow your spirit, and upon this charge
Cry 'God for Harry, England, and Saint George!'.

King Henry—Henry V III.i

From camp to camp through the foul womb of night
The hum of either army stilly sounds,
That the fix'd sentinels almost receive
The secret whispers of each other's watch:
Fire answers fire, and through their paly flames
Each battle sees the other's umber'd face;
Steed threatens steed, in high and boastful neighs
Piercing the night's dull ear; and from the tents
The armourers, accomplishing the knights,
With busy hammers closing rivets up,
Give dreadful note of preparation:

Chorus—Henry V IV.Prologue

O God of battles! steel my soldiers' hearts,
Possess them not with fear; take from them now
The sense of reck'ning, if th' oppos'd numbers
Pluck their hearts from them.   *King Henry—Henry V IV.i*

This day is call'd the feast of Crispian:
He that outlives this day, and comes safe home,
Will stand a tip-toe when this day is nam'd,
And rouse him at the name of Crispian.
He that shall see this day, and live old age,
Will yearly on the vigil feast his neighbours,
And say 'Tomorrow is Saint Crispian.'
Then will he strip his sleeve and show his scars,
And say 'These wounds I had on Crispin's day.'
Old men forget; yet all shall be forgot,
But he'll remember with advantages
What feats he did that day: then shall our names
Familiar in his mouth as household words,
Harry the king, Bedford and Exeter,
Warwick and Talbot, Salisbury and Gloucester,
Be in their flowing cups freshly rememb'red.
This story shall the good man teach his son;
And Crispin Crispian shall ne'er go by,
From this day to the ending of the world,
But we in it shall be remembered;
We few, we happy few, we band of brothers;
For he today that sheds his blood with me
Shall be my brother; be he ne'er so vile,
This day shall gentle his condition:
And gentlemen in England now a-bed
Shall think themselves accurs'd they were not here,
And hold their manhoods cheap whiles any speaks
That fought with us upon Saint Crispin's day.
                King Henry—Henry V IV.iii

And as our vineyards, fallows, meads and hedges,
Defective in their natures, grow to wildness,
Even so our houses and ourselves and children
Have lost, or do not learn for want of time,
The sciences that should become our country;
But grow like savages—as soldiers will
That nothing do but meditate on blood—
To swearing and stern looks, diffus'd attire
And everything that seems unnatural.

Burgundy—Henry V V.ii

'Tis the soldiers' life
To have their balmy slumbers wak'd with strife.

Othello—Othello II.iii

Who does i' th' wars more than his captain can
Becomes his captain's captain: and ambition,
The soldier's virtue, rather makes choice of loss,
Than gain which darkens him.   Ventidius—A&C III.i

Honour and policy, like unsever'd friends,
I' th' war do grow together.   Volumnia—Coriolanus III.ii

Save thyself;
For friends kill friends, and the disorder's such
As war were hoodwink'd.   Lucius—Cymbeline V.ii

WEALTH: "What's ought, but as 'tis valued?"

An I had but one penny in the world, thou shouldst have it
to buy gingerbread: hold, there is the very remuneration I
had of thy master, thou halfpenny purse of wit, thou
pigeon-egg of discretion.   Costard—LLL V.i

Nothing comes amiss, so money comes withal.

Grumio—TS I.ii

Our purses shall be proud, our garments poor;
For 'tis the mind that makes the body rich.

Petruchio—TS IV.iii

Well, whiles I am a beggar, I will rail
And say there is no sin but to be rich;
And being rich, my virtue then shall be
To say there is no vice but beggary.   *Bastard—King John II.i*

Bell, book, and candle shall not drive me back,
When gold and silver becks me to come on.

Bastard—King John III.iii

There is thy gold, worse poison to men's souls,
Doing more murder in this loathsome world,
Than these poor compounds that thou mayst not sell.
I sell thee poison, thou hast sold me none.   *Romeo—RJ V.i*

And yet, for aught I see, they are as sick that surfeit with too
much as they that starve with nothing. It is no mean happiness therefore, to be seated in the mean; superfluity comes
sooner by white hairs, but competency lives longer.

Nerissa—MV I.ii

Men that hazard all
Do it in hope of fair advantages.   *Morocco—MV II.vii*

All that glisters is not gold;
Often have you heard that told:
Many a man his life hath sold

But my outside to behold:
Gilded tombs do worms infold.   *Morocco—MV II.vii*

This making of Christians will raise the price of hogs; if we
grow all to be pork-eaters, we shall not shortly have a
rasher on the coals for money.   *Launcelot—MV III.v*

For, they say, if money go before, all ways do lie open.
Ford—Merry Wives II.ii

Wooing thee, I found thee of more value
Than stamps in gold or sums in sealed bags.
Fenton—Merry Wives III.iv

O, what a world of vile ill-favour'd faults
Looks handsome in three hundred pounds a-year!
Anne—Merry Wives III.iv

To have seen much and to have nothing, is to have rich eyes
and poor hands.   *Rosalind—AYLI IV.i*

Youth is bought more oft than begg'd or borrow'd.
Olivia—TN III.iv

What's aught, but as 'tis valued?
Troilus—TC II.ii

But value dwells not in particular will;
It holds his estimate and dignity
As well wherein 'tis precious of itself
As in the prizer;   *Hector—TC II.ii*

You do as chapmen do,
Dispraise the thing that you desire to buy:

But we in silence hold this virtue well,
We'll not commend what we intend to sell.   *Paris—TC IV.i*

To the noble mind
Rich gifts wax poor when givers prove unkind.
Ophelia—Hamlet III.i

And this is all a liberal course allows;
Who cannot keep his wealth must keep his house.
Servant—Timon III.iii

O, the fierce wretchedness that glory brings us!
Who would not wish to be from wealth exempt,
Since riches point to misery and contempt?
Flavius—Timon IV.ii

'Tis gold
Which buys admittance; oft it doth; yea, and makes
Diana's rangers false themselves, yield up
Their deer to th' stand o' th' stealer; and 'tis gold
Which makes the true man kill'd and saves the thief;
Nay, sometime hangs both thief and true man: what
Can it not do and undo?   *Cloten—Cymbeline II.iii*

All gold and silver turn to dirt!
As 'tis no better reckon'd, but of those
Who worship dirty gods.   *Arviragus—Cymbeline III.vi*

You pay a great deal too dear for what's given freely.
Camillo—WT I.i

Though authority be a stubborn bear, yet he is oft led by the
nose with gold; show the inside of your purse to the outside
of his hand, and no more ado.   *Clown—WT IV.iv*

WISE WORDS: "The world's mine oyster"

They say every why hath a wherefore.
                              Dromio—CE II.ii

Faith, as you say, there's small choice in rotten apples.
                              Hortensio—TS I.i

Pitchers have ears.
                              Baptista—TS IV.iv
                 QueenElizabeth—Richard III II.iv

He that is giddy thinks the world turns round.
                              Widow—TS V.ii

A subtle traitor needs no sophister.
                              Queen—2 Henry VI V.i

Patience is for poltroons.
                              Clifford—3 Henry VI I.i

Much rain wears the marble.
                 Gloucester—3 Henry VI III.ii

In common worldly things, 'tis call'd ungrateful,
With dull unwillingness to repay a debt
Which with a bounteous hand was kindly lent.
                 Dorset—Richard III II.ii

True hope is swift, and flies with swallow's wings;
Kings it makes gods, and meaner creatures kings.
                 Richmond—Richard III V.ii

Sir, sir, impatience hath his privilege.

Pembroke—King John IV.iii

What, man! more water glideth by the mill
Than wots the miller of; and easy it is
Of a cut loaf to steal a shive, we know.

Demetrius—Titus II.i

For the bawdy hand of the dial is now upon the prick of
noon.   *Mercutio—RJ II.iv*

Marry, sir, 'tis an ill cook that cannot lick his own fingers.

Servant—RJ IV.ii

The brain may devise laws for the blood, but a hot temper
leaps o'er a cold decree; such a hare is madness the youth,
to skip o'er the meshes of good counsel the cripple.

Portia—MV I.ii

All things that are,
Are with more spirit chased than enjoy'd.

Gratiano—MV II.vi

Comparisons are odorous.

Dogberry—Much Ado III.v

Why, then the world's mine oyster,
Which I with sword will open.   *Pistol—Merry Wives II.ii*

They say there is divinity in odd numbers, either in nativity,
chance or death.   *Falstaff—Merry Wives V.i*

Against such lewdsters and their lechery
Those that betray them do no treachery.

Mrs. Page—Merry Wives V.ii

Omittance is no quittance.
Phoebe—AYLI III.v

He that is well hanged in this world needs to fear no colours.
Feste—TN I.v

Be not afraid of greatness: some are born great, some achieve greatness, and some have greatness thrust upon 'em.
Malvolio—TN II.v

They love not poison that do poison need.
Bolingbroke—Richard II V.vi

Though patience be a tired mare, yet she will plod.
Corporal Nym—Henry V II.i

Indeed, it is a strange-disposed time;
But men may construe things after their fashion,
Clean from the purpose of the things themselves.
Cicero—JC I.iii

Those that with haste will make a mighty fire
Begin it with weak straws.
Cassius—JC I.iii

O hateful error, melancholy's child,
Why dost thou show to the apt thoughts of men
The things that are not? O error, soon conceiv'd,
Thou never com'st unto a happy birth,
But kill'st the mother that engend'red thee!
Messenger—JC V.iii

If you love an addle egg as well as you love an idle head, you would eat chickens i' the shell.
Cressida—TC I.ii

Light boats sail swift, though greater hulks draw deep.

Agamemnon—TC II.iii

How the devil Luxury, with his fat rump and potato-finger,
tickles these together! Fry, lechery, fry!   *Thersites—TC V.ii*

I am but mad north-north-west: when the wind is southerly
I know a hawk from a handsaw.   *Hamlet—Hamlet II.ii*

She that's a maid now, and laughs at my departure,
Shall not be a maid long, unless things be cut shorter.

Fool—Lear I.v

Now a little fire in a wild field were like an old lecher's
heart; a small spark, all the rest on 's body cold.

Fool—Lear III.iv

Jesters do oft prove prophets.

Regan—Lear V.iii

Pity's sleeping:
Strange times, that weep with laughing, not with weeping!

Timon—Timon IV.iii

Much drink may be said to be an equivocator with lechery;
it makes him, and it mars him; it sets him on, and it takes
him off; it persuades him, and disheartens him; makes him
stand to, and not stand to; in conclusion, equivocates him in
a sleep, and giving him the lie, leaves him.

Porter—Macbeth II.iii

Much is breeding,
Which, like the courser's hair, hath yet but life,
And not a serpent's poison.   *Antony—A&C I.ii*

Who seeks, and will not take when once 'tis offer'd,
Shall never find it more.   *Menas—A&C II.vii*

They say poor suitors have strong breaths—they shall know
we have strong arms too.   *First Citizen—Coriolanus I.i*

One fire drives out one fire; one nail, one nail;
Rights by rights falter, strengths by strengths do fail.
                              Aufidius—Coriolanus IV.vii

Who makes the fairest show means most deceit.
                              Cleon—Pericles I.iv

You smell this business with a sense as cold
As is a dead man's nose.   *Leontes—WT II.i*

A beggar's book
Outworths a noble's blood.   *Buckingham—Henry VIII I.i*

But all hoods make not monks.
                              Katharine—Henry VIII III.i

WITS AND FOOLS: "Your wits make wise things foolish"

There's many a man hath more hair than wit.
                      Antipholus of Syracuse—CE II.ii

Your wit's too hot, it speeds too fast, 'twill tire.
                              Berowne—LLL II.i

Good wits will be jangling.
                              Rosaline—LLL II.i

Folly in fools bears not so strong a note
As foolery in the wise, when wit doth dote;
Since all the power thereof it doth apply
To prove, by wit, worth in simplicity. *Maria—LLL V.ii*

A jest's prosperity lies in the ear
Of him that hears it, never in the tongue
Of him that makes it. *Rosaline—LLL V.ii*

Homekeeping youth have ever homely wits.
Valentine—TGV I.i

Lord, what fools these mortals be!
Puck—MND III.ii

Thy wit is a very bitter sweeting; it is a most sharp sauce.
Mercutio—RJ II.iv

O, here's a wit of cheveril, that stretches fron an inch narrow to an ell broad! *Mercutio—RJ II.iv*

O, these deliberate fools! when they do choose,
They have the wisdom by their wit to lose.
Portia—MV II.viii

Goodly Lord, what a wit-snapper are you!
Lorenzo—MV III.v

What a pretty thing man is when he goes in his doublet and
hose and leaves off his wit! *Beatrice—Much Ado V.i*

Thy wit is as quick as the greyhound's mouth; it catches.
Beatrice—Much Ado V.ii

The more pity, that fools may not speak wisely what wise
men do foolishly.   *Touchstone—AYLI I.ii*

Thou sayest true; for since the little wit that fools have was
silenced, the little foolery that wise men have makes a great
show.   *Celia—AYLI I.ii*

He that a fool doth very wisely hit
Doth very foolishly, though he do smart,
Not so seem senseless of the bob: if not,
The wise man's folly is anatomized
Even by the squand'ring glances of the fool.
                                     Jacques—AYLI II.vii

All's brave that youth mounts and folly guides.
                                     Celia—AYLI III.iv

I had rather have a fool to make me merry than experience
to make me sad.   *Rosalind—AYLI IV.i*

I do now remember a saying: 'The fool doth think he is
wise, but the wise man knows himself to be a fool.' The
heathen philosopher, when he had a desire to eat a grape,
would open his lips when he put it into his mouth; meaning
thereby that grapes were made to eat and lips to open.
                                     Touchstone—AYLI V.i

Wit, an 't be thy will, put me into a good fooling! Those
wits, that think they have thee, do very oft prove fools; and
I, that am sure I lack thee, may pass for a wise man: for
what says Quinapalus? 'Better a witty fool than a foolish
wit.'   *Feste—TN I.v*

There is no slander in an allowed fool, though he do nothing but rail; nor no railing in a known discreet man, though he do nothing but reprove.   *Olivia—TN I.v*

To see this age! A sentence is but a cheveril glove to a good wit: how quickly the wrong side may be turned outward!
                                                                Feste—TN III.i

Fools are as like husbands as pilchers are to herrings; the husband's the bigger.   *Feste—TN III.i*

Foolery, sir, does walk about the orb like the sun, it shines everywhere.   *Feste—TN III.i*

This fellow is wise enough to play the fool;
And to do that well craves a kind of wit;
He must observe their mood on whom he jests,
The quality of persons, and the time,
And, like the haggard, check at every feather
That comes before his eye. This is a practice
As full of labour as a wise man's art:
For folly that he wisely shows is fit;
But wise men, folly-fall'n, quite taint their wit.
                                                                Viola—TN III.i

These wise men that give fools money get themselves a good report—after fourteen years' purchase.
                                                                Feste—TN IV.i

I am not only witty in myself, but the cause that wit is in other men.   *Falstaff—2 Henry IV I.ii*

This rudeness is a sauce to his good wit,
Which gives men stomach to digest his words
With better appetite.   *Brutus—JC I.ii*

O heaven, the vanity of wretched fools!
Duke—MforM V.i

The common curse of mankind, folly and ingnorance, be thine in great revenue!
Thersites—TC II.iii

The amity that wisdon knits not, folly may easily untie.
Ulysses—TC II.iii

Brevity is the soul of wit.
Polonius—Hamlet II.ii

Thou know'st we work by wit, and not by witchcraft;
And wit depends on dilatory time.   *Iago—Othello II.iii*

Fools had ne're less grace in a year;
    For wise men are grown foppish,
And know mot how their wits to wear,
    Their manners are so apish.   *Fool—Lear I.iv*

We call a nettle but a nettle and
The faults of fools but folly.   *Menenius—Coriolanus II.i*

Fools are not mad folks.
Imogen—Cymbeline II.iii

Look, he's winding up the watch of his wit; by and by it will strike.   *Sebastian—Tempest II.i*

WOMANHOOD: "Frailty, thy name is woman!"

Alas, poor women! Make us but believe,
    Being compact of credit, that you love us;

Though others have the arm, show us the sleeve;
  We in your motion turn, and you may move us.
                                    Luciana—CE III.ii

The venom clamors of a jealous woman
  Poisons more deadly than a mad dog's tooth.
                                    Abbess—CE V.i

If she be made of white and red,
  Her faults will ne'er be known
For blushing cheeks by faults are bred,
  And fears by pale white shown:
Then if she fear, or be to blame,
  By this you shall not know,
For still her cheeks possess the same
  Which native she doth owe.   *Moth—LLL I.ii*

Your mistresses dare never come in rain,
For fear their colours should be wash'd away.
                                    Berowne—LLL IV.iii

The tongues of mocking wenches are as keen
  As is the razor's edge invisible,
Cutting a smaller hair than may be seen,
  Above the sense of sense.   *Boyet—LLL V.ii*

Fair ladies mask'd are roses in their bud;
Dismask'd, their damask sweet commixture shown,
Are angels vailing clouds, or roses blown.   *Boyet—LLL V.ii*

I have no other but a woman's reason; I think him so because I think him so.   *Lucetta—TGV I.ii*

Dumb jewels often in their silent kind
More than quick words do move a woman's mind.

Valentine—TGV III.i

'Item: She hath more hair than wit, and more faults than
hairs, and more wealth than faults.'   *Speed—TGV III.i*

It is the lesser blot, modesty finds,
Women to change their shapes than men their minds.

Julia—TGV V.iv

I see a woman may be made a fool,
If she had not a spirit to resist.   *Katherine—TS III.ii*

Kindness in women, not their beauteous looks,
Shall win my love.   *Hortensio—TS IV.ii*

A woman mov'd is like a fountain troubled,
Muddy, ill-seeming, thick, bereft of beauty;
And while it is so, none so dry or thirsty
Will deign to sip or touch one drop of it.
Thy husband is thy lord, thy life, thy keeper,
Thy head, thy sovereign; one that cares for thee,
And for thy maintenance commits his body
To painful labour both by sea and land;
To watch the night in storms, the day in cold,
Whilst thou li'st warm at home, secure and safe;
And craves no other tribute at thy hands
But love, fair looks, and true obedience;
Too little payment for so great a debt.
Such duty as the subject owes the prince
Even such a woman oweth to her husband;
And when she is froward, peevish, sullen, sour,

And not obedient to his honest will,
What is she but a foul contending rebel
And graceless traitor to her loving lord?
I am ashamed that women are so simple
To offer war when they should kneel for peace,
Or seek for rule, supremacy and sway,
When they are bound to serve, love and obey.

Katherine—TS V.ii

For when a world of men
Could not prevail with all their oratory,
Yet hath a woman's kindness over-rul'd.

Talbot—1 Henry VI II.ii

'Tis beauty that doth oft make women proud;
But, God he knows, thy share thereof is small:
'Tis virtue that doth make them most admir'd;
The contrary doth make thee wond'red at;
'Tis government that makes them seem divine;
The want thereof makes them abominable:
Thou are as opposite to every good
As the Antipodes are unto us;
Or as the south to the septentrion.
O tiger's heart wrapt in a woman's hide!

York—3 Henry VI I.iv

She's beautiful and therefore to be woo'd;
She is a woman, therefore to be won.

Suffolk—1 Henry VI V.iii

A woman's general; what should we fear?

Richard—3 Henry VI I.ii

He that perforce robs lions of their hearts
May easily win a woman's.   *Bastard—King John I.i*

Women, being the weaker vessels, are ever thrust to the
wall.   *Samson—RJ I.i*

Women may fall, when there's no strength in men.
                    Friar Laurence—RJ II.iii

The wiser, the waywarder: make the doors upon a woman's
wit and it will out at the casement; shut that and 'twill out
at the keyhole; stop that, and 'twill fly with the smoke out at
the chimney.   *Rosalind—AYLI IV.i*

O, that woman that cannot make her fault her husband's
occasion, let her never nurse her child herself, for she will
breed it like a fool!   *Rosalind—AYLI IV.i*

How easy is it for the proper-false
In women's waxen hearts to set their forms!
Alas, our frailty is the cause, not we!
For such as we are made of, such we be.   *Viola—TN II.ii*

For women are as roses, whose fair flow'r
Being once display'd, doth fall that very hour.
                    Orsino—TN II.iv

Be merry, be merry, my wife has all;
For women are shrews, both short and tall:
'Tis merry in hall when bears wag all,
And welcome merry Shrove-tide.   *Silence—2 Henry IV V.iii*

Maids, well summered and warm kept, are like flies at
Bartholomew-tide, blind, though they have their eyes; and

then they will endure handling, which before would not
abide looking on.   *Burgundy—Henry V V.ii*

How hard it is for women to keep counsel!
                                     Portia—JC II.iv

Ay me, how weak a thing
The heart of woman is!   *Portia—JC II.iv*

When maidens sue,
Men give like gods; but when they weep and kneel,
All their petitions are as freely theirs
As they themselves would owe them.   *Lucio—MforM I.iv*

Women! Help Heaven! men their creation mar
In profiting by them. Nay, call us ten times frail;
For we are soft as our complexions are,
And credulous to false prints.   *Isabella—MforM II.iv*

Women are light at midnight.
                                     Lucio—MforM V.i

Women are angels, wooing:
Things won are done; joy's soul lies in the doing.
That she belov'd knows nought that knows not this:
Men prize the thing ungain'd more than it is:
That she was never yet that ever knew
Love got so sweet as when desire did sue.
Therefore this maxim out of love I teach:
Achievement is command; ungain'd, beseech:
                                     Cressida—TC I.ii

A woman impudent and mannish grown
Is not more loath'd than an effeminate man
In time of action.   *Patroclus—TC III.iii*

O , these encounterers, so glib of tongue,
That give a coasting welcome ere it comes,
And wide unclasp the tables of their thoughts
To every ticklish reader! set them down
For sluttish spoils of opportunity
And daughters of the game.   *Ulysses—TC IV.v*

Ah, poor our sex! this fault in us I find,
The error of our eye directs our mind:
What error leads must err; O, then conclude
Minds sway'd by eyes are full of turpitude.
                                    Cressida—TC V.ii

Let it not be believ'd for womanhood!
                                    Troilus—TC V.ii

I have heard of your paintings too, well enough; God hath
given you one face, and you make yourselves another: you
jig, you amble, and you lisp; you nick-name God's creatures, and make your wantonness your ignorance.
                                    Hamlet—Hamlet III.i

Come on, come on; you are pictures out of doors,
Bells in your parlours, wild-cats in your kitchens,
Saints in your injuries, devils being offended,
Players in your housewifery, and housewives in your beds.
                                    Iago—Othello II.i

See thyself, devil!
Proper deformity seems not in the fiend
So horrid as in woman.   *Albany—Lear IV.ii*

Age cannot wither her, nor custom stale
Her infinite variety; other women cloy
The appetites they feed; but she makes hungry

Where most she satisfies: for vilest things
Become themselves in her; that the holy priests
Bless her when she is riggish.   *Enobarbus—A&C II.ii*

But there is never a fair woman has a true face.
          Enobarbus—A&C II.vi

Women are not
In their best fortunes strong; but want will perjure
The ne'er-touched vestal.   *Caesar—A&C III.xii*

Faith, she would serve after a long voyage at sea.
          Lysimachus—Pericles IV.vi

Her beauty and her brain go not together; she's a good sign,
but I have seen small reflection of her wit.
          First Lord—Cymbeline I.ii

She shines not upon fools, lest the reflection should hurt
her.   *First Lord—Cymbeline I.ii*

Let there be no honour
Where there is beauty; truth, where semblance; love,
Where there's another man; the vows of women
Of no more bondage be, to where they are made,
Than they are to their virtues; which is nothing.
          Posthumus—Cymbeline II.iv

For there's no motion
That tends to vice in man, but I affirm
It is the woman's part: be it lying, note it,
The woman's; flattering, hers; deceiving, hers;
Lust and rank thoughts, hers, hers; revenges, hers;
Ambitions, covetings, change of prides, disdain,
Nice longing, slanders, mutability,

All faults that may be nam'd, nay, that hell knows,
Why, hers, in part or all; but rather, all;
For even to vice
They are not constant, but are changing still
One vice, but of a minute old, for one
Not half so old as that. I'll write against them,
Detest them, curse them: yet 'tis greater skill
In a true hate, to pray they have their will:
The very devils cannot plague them better.

Posthumus—Cymbeline II.v

Two women plac'd together makes cold weather.

Chamberlain—Henry VIII I.iv

INDEX